William James Ashley, Fustel de Coulanges

The Origin of Property in Land Translated by Margaret Ashley

With an Introductory Chapter on the English manor by W.J. Ashley

William James Ashley, Fustel de Coulanges

The Origin of Property in Land Translated by Margaret Ashley
With an Introductory Chapter on the English manor by W.J. Ashley

ISBN/EAN: 9783337130572

Printed in Europe, USA, Canada, Australia, Japan

Cover: Foto ©Suzi / pixelio.de

More available books at **www.hansebooks.com**

THE ORIGIN OF PROPERTY IN LAND

BY

FUSTEL DE COULANGES

TRANSLATED BY MARGARET ASHLEY

WITH AN INTRODUCTORY CHAPTER ON

THE ENGLISH MANOR

BY

W. J. ASHLEY, M.A.

PROFESSOR OF POLITICAL ECONOMY IN THE UNIVERSITY OF TORONTO,
LATE FELLOW OF LINCOLN COLLEGE, OXFORD

LONDON
SWAN SONNENSCHEIN & CO.
PATERNOSTER SQUARE
1891

PREFACE.

THE Essay by the late M. Fustel de Coulanges, here translated, appeared in the *Revue des Questions Historiques* for April, 1889. It seemed especially suitable for translation; since it presented in a comparatively brief compass all the main arguments of that great historian against the various attempts which have been made to support the theory of primitive agrarian communism by an appeal to historical records. The translation has been made with the consent of Madame Fustel de Coulanges; and it has benefited by the suggestions of M. Guiraud, an old pupil of the author, and now "Chargé de Cours" at the Sorbonne. The presentation of the Essay in an English dress has been deemed a suitable occasion to estimate the bearing of its arguments on early English social history, and to review in the light of it the evidence now accessible as to the origin of the English manor.

W. J. A.
M. A.

TORONTO,
January 21, 1891.

CONTENTS.

INTRODUCTORY CHAPTER.

THE ENGLISH MANOR.

In spite of all the labour that has been spent on the early history of England, scholars are at variance upon the most fundamental of questions: the question whether that history began with a population of independent freemen or with a population of dependent serfs. Nothing less than this is at issue in the current discussions as to the existence of the "mark" and the origin of the manor; as well as in the discussions, at first sight of less significance, as to the character of our mediæval constitution. Neither for the government of the parish nor for the government of the nation is it possible to construct an historical theory which does not rest, consciously or unconsciously, on some view as to the position of the body of the people.

The opinion almost universally accepted four or five years ago was to this effect: that the English people, when it came to Britain, was composed of a stalwart host of free men, who governed themselves by popular national councils, administered justice by popular local assemblies, and lived together in little village groups of independent yeomen. It was, indeed, recognised that there were gradations of rank—*eorl* and *ceorl*, and the like,—and that some indi-

viduals were unfortunate enough to be slaves. But
these and similar facts were not supposed to affect the
general outlines of the picture; and even those writers
who expressed themselves most guardedly as to this
"primitive Teutonic polity," proceeded by the subsequent course of their narrative to assume it as their
starting point. And looking back on the intellectual
history of the last fifty years, we can easily trace the
forces which assisted in giving this view currency.
To begin with, the historical movement of this century was undoubtedly the offspring of Romanticism;
and with Romanticism the noble independence of the
unlettered barbarian was an article of faith. Moreover, the discovery of modern constitutionalism "in
the forests of Germany" harmonised with a comfort-
able belief, which was at one time very common.
This was the belief to which Kingsley gave such
eloquent expression, that the barbarian invasions
were the predestined means of bringing into the
effete civilisation of Rome the manly virtues of the
North. For England the theory had the additional
charm, during a period of democratic change, of satis-
fying that most unscientific but most English desire,
the desire for precedent. An extension of the suffrage
rose far above mere expediency when it became a
reconquest of primitive rights.

But, though we can understand how it was that
historians came to discover the imposing figure of the

free Teuton, it does not necessarily follow that they
were mistaken. The disproof must be accomplished,
if at all, by erudition equal to that by which the
doctrine has been supported; and it has been the
task of M. Fustel de Coulanges to assail with enormous learning and a cogent style almost every one of
those propositions as to early mediæval constitutional
history, which we were beginning to deem the secure
achievements of German science.

There was a great contrast, both in their character
and in the reception afforded to them, between the
earlier and the later works of M. Fustel. He gained
his reputation, in 1864, by his *Cité Antique*, a book
wherein, unlike his later insistence on the complexity
of institutions, he used one simple idea—that of the
religion of the family—to solve most of the problems
presented by ancient civilisation. It gained immediately an extraordinary success; especially in England,
where it fell in with all that current of thought
which was then beginning to turn into the direction
of social evolution, comparative politics, and the like.
For a year or so, the final piece of advice which
schoolmasters gave to men who were going up for
scholarships at the Universities was to read the *Cité
Antique.*

Then for several years M. Fustel was not heard from,
at any rate in England; although it might have been
seen by occasional articles in the *Revue des Deux Mondes*

and elsewhere that he was devoting himself to the early Middle Ages. In 1875 appeared the first volume of a *Histoire des Institutions politiques de l'ancienne France*, reaching to the end of the Merovingian period. But further investigation and the controversy to which the book gave rise made him resolve to go over the ground again more minutely in a series of volumes. Meanwhile he issued in 1885 his *Recherches sur quelques problèmes d'histoire*. With the modest declaration that before attempting to write the history of feudalism—"un corps infiniment vaste, à organes multiples, à faces changeantes, à vie complexe "—it was necessary to consider some preliminary questions, he threw down the gauntlet to the dominant school. He challenged the whole theory of primitive German life which was fondly supposed to rest on the authority of Cæsar and Tacitus; he showed how little evidence there was for the supposed existence of popular courts of justice; he traced the growth of the class of *coloni* or semi-servile peasants under the later Roman empire, in a way which suggested that they must have played a far more important part in subsequent social development than is usually assigned to them ; and, finally, he denied altogether the existence of that free, self-governing village community with common ownership of the village lands, which Maurer had made familiar to us as the *mark*. His antagonism to German scholars was evidently

sharpened by national antipathy: like his country-
men in many other departments of science, he was
bent on proving that France could beat Germany
with its own peculiar instruments of patient scholarship and minute research. It is turning the tables
with a vengeance, when the Frenchman shakes his
head, with much apparent reason, over the inexplic-
able rashness of his German brethren.

Having thus cleared the way, M. Fustel began to
put together his materials for the great work of his life,
the *Histoire des Institutions Politiques*, in its new
form. He had issued one volume and prepared for
publication a second when he was prematurely lost to
the world. His pupils have, indeed, been able to put
together a third volume from his manuscript and from
earlier articles; and a fourth and fifth are promised
us. But these fragmentary sketches, written many of
them under the shadow of approaching death, are only
slight indications of what M. Fustel might have done
for mediæval history. Nevertheless, his work, incomplete as it is, is of the utmost weight and significance;
in my opinion, it has done more than that of any
other scholar to bring back the study of mediæval
society, after long aberrations, to the right lines. We
have to continue the work of inquiry along these
lines, and in his spirit. "It is now," said he, in the
Preface to the *Recherches*, "twenty-five years since I
began to teach; and each year I have had the happi-

ness to have four or five pupils. What I have taught
them above everything else has been to *inquire*.
What I have impressed upon them is not to believe
everything easy, and never to pass by problems without seeing them. The one truth of which I have
persistently endeavoured to convince them is that
history is the most difficult of sciences." And again,
in the Introduction to *L'Alleu*, "Of late years
people have invented the word *sociology*. The word
history had the same sense and meant the same thing,
at least for those who understood it. History is the
science of social facts; that is to say, it is sociology
itself." "The motto he had chosen, a motto," says
one of his pupils, "which sums up his whole scientific
life, was *Quaero*."

It is curious to observe how slow English scholars
have been to realise the importance of these recent
volumes. Is it because theories of mediæval history,
which are not more than twenty or thirty years
old, have already hardened into dogma, and we
shrink from the reconstruction which might be necessary were we to meddle with any of the corner-stones?
Some consolation, however, may be found in the fact
that a considerable effect has been produced by the
work of an English investigator, who was quite inde-
pendently arriving, though from a different point of
view, at very similar conclusions. Mr. Seebohm's
English Village Community, it is no exaggeration to

way, revealed to us, for the first time, the inner life of
mediæval England. By making us realise not only
how uniform was the manorial system over the
greater part of England, but also how burdensome
were the obligations of the tenants, it forced us to
reconsider the accepted explanation of its origin.
For the explanation generally accepted was that
manors had come into existence piecemeal, by the
gradual subjection, here in one way, there in another, of
the free landowners to their more powerful neighbours.
Mr. Seebohm made it appear probable that the lord of
the manor, instead of being a late intruder, was from
the first, so far as England was concerned, the owner
of the soil and the lord of those who tilled it; that
the development has been in the main and from the
first an advance from servitude to freedom; and not
an elevation after long centuries of increasing de-
gradation.

Mr. Seebohm has not, perhaps, been so convincing
in the explanation he has to offer of the origin
of the manor; but there is now a marked tendency to
accept what is, after all, his main contention—that the
manorial system was in existence, not as an exceptional phenomenon, but as the prevailing form of social
organisation very soon, at any rate, after the English
Conquest. There is absolutely no clear documentary
evidence for the free village community in England.
As to the word *mark*, not even Kemble, who first in-

troduced it to English readers, could produce an
example of its use in English documents in the sense
of land owned by a community; and Anglo-Saxon
scholars now point out that his one doubtful instance
of *mearemót* [A.D. 971] and his three examples of
mearcbeorh are most naturally explained as having to
do with *mark* merely in the sense of a boundary.[1]
Not only is there no early evidence; the arguments
based on supposed survivals into later times seem to
melt away on close examination. It has, for instance,
been maintained that even in the Domesday Survey
there are traces of free communities. But the supposed Domesday references are of the scantiest, and
certainly would not suggest the mark to anyone who
was not looking for it. Most of them seem easily
susceptible of other interpretations; in some of them
we probably have to do with two or three joint-
owners, in others very possibly with villages where
the lord has been bought out.[2] Another and more
usual argument is derived from the Court Baron,
which was described by later legal theory as absolutely essential to a manor, and yet of such a constitution that it could not be held unless there were at
least two free tenants to attend it. But legal his-

[1] Earle, *Land Charters*, p. xlv.
[2] Cf. Southbydyk in *Boldon Book*, Domesday, iv. 568; and
Nasse's remarks (*Agricultural Community*, p. 46) as to cases of
purchase in Mecklenburg.

torians are beginning to regard the Court Baron as
not at all primitive, but rather as a comparatively late
outcome of feudal theory.[1]

It must be granted that there is little direct evidence prior to the 9th century in disproof of the free
community; but all the indirect evidence seems to tell
against it. Gibbon long ago pointed out that the
grant by the King of the South Saxons to St. Wilfrid,
in the year 680, of the peninsula of Selsey (described
as "the land of 87 families"), with the persons and
property of all its inhabitants, showed that there, at
any rate, there was a dependent population; especially
as Bede goes on to tell us that among these inhabitants there were 250 slaves. And there are two
still more considerable pieces of evidence to which
due attention has hardly been given. The one is that
the great majority of the early grants of land, beginning as early as 674, expressly transfer with the soil
the cultivators upon it, and speak of them by precisely
the same terms, *casati* and *mancentes*, as were in contemporary use on the Continent to designate praedial
serfs.[2] The other is that, as in the rest of Western
Europe the whole country was divided into *villae*,
each *villa* being a domain belonging to one or more

[1] See Maitland, *Select Pleas in Manorial Courts*, Introduction;
and also in *Engl. Hist. Rev.*, 1898, p. 568; Blakesley, in *Law
Quarterly Rev.*, 1889, p. 113.

[2] Abundant instances in Earle, *Land Charters*; cf. Fustel de
Coulanges, *L'Alleu*, p. 377.

proprietors, and cultivated by more or less servile
tenants,[1] so in Bede's *Ecclesiastical History*, written
in 731, the ordinary local division is also *villa*, often
specifically described as *villa regia* or *villa comitis*.
He does indeed use *vicus* or *viculus* a dozen times ;
but in three of these cases the word *regis* or *regius* is
added, and in two the term *villa* is also used in
the same chapter for the same place.[2] These five
examples, it may further be noticed, occur in a narrative of the events of the middle of the seventh century,
—a period near enough to Bede's own time for his
evidence to be valuable, and yet within a century and
a half after the conquest of the districts in question.

The absence, however, of direct evidence in proof of
the original free community in England, and the presence of much indirect evidence in its disproof, have
hitherto been supposed to be counterbalanced by the
well-ascertained existence of the mark among our German kinsfolk, and by the results of " the comparative
method," especially as applied to India.   Let us take
the *markgenossenschaft* first.   It is a little difficult
to discover the exact relation between Kemble and

---

[1] See Fustel de Coulanges, *L'Alleu.* ch. vi.

[2] *Hist. Eccl.*, iii., 17, 21, 22, 28. The use of the word *township* and its relation to *villa* require fresh examination in the
light of our increased knowledge of Continental usage. *Tunscip*
apparently first appears in Alfred's translation of Bede, at the
end of the ninth century ; and its first and only appearance in
A.S. law is in Edgar iv. 8, in the second half of the tenth.
Schmid, *Gesetze der Angelsachen, Gloss. s. v.*

Maurer; but the obvious supposition is that it was from Maurer that Kemble derived his main ideas; and it has usually been supposed that however Kemble may have exaggerated the action of the mark in England, in Germany it could be traced with un-hesitating certainty. This is what, to Englishmen, gives especial interest to the essay of M. Fustel de Coulanges translated in the present volume.

M. Fustel begins with the ironical announce-ment that he does not intend to criticise the theory of the mark in itself, but only to examine the document-ary evidence alleged in its favour, and to determine whether such evidence can fairly be given the con-struction that Maurer puts upon it. But here M. Fustel does some injustice to himself; for in following a detailed criticism of this character the reader is apt to overlook or forget the really important points which the writer succeeds in establishing. It may be well to state these points in our own way and order, as follows: (1) That the mark theory de-rives no direct support from the language of Cæsar and Tacitus; (2) That the word *mark* in early German law means primarily a boundary, usually the bound-ary of a private property; and then, in a derivative sense, the property itself, a domain such as in Gaul was called a *villa*; (3) That early German law is throughout based on the assumption of private pro-perty in land, and never upon that of common ownership, whether by a whole people or by a village group; and that whatever traces there may be of earlier conditions point to rights possessed by the *family* and not by any larger body; (4) That the one direct proof of a custom of periodical redistribution of the village lands is derived from an evident blunder on the part of a copyist; and that the rest of the evidence has nothing at all to do with periodical divisions; (5) That the term *common* as applied to fields and woods in early German law means common to, or shared by two or more individual owners; (6) That the *commons, allmende, common of wood* and similar phrases, which occur frequently in documents of the ninth and succeeding centuries, point to a customary right of use enjoyed by tenants over land belonging to a lord; and that there is no evidence that the tenants were once joint *owners* of the land over which they enjoyed such rights; (7) That there is no evidence in the early Middle Ages of mark assemblies or mark courts; and finally, the most important point of all, (8) That to judge from the earliest German codes, great states cultivated by slaves or by various grades of semi-servile tenants were the rule rather than the exception even at the beginning of the Middle Ages. Professor Lamprecht, whom M. Fustel treats as a mere follower of Maurer, is naturally sore at the treatment he here receives; and indeed his great work on German economic history is of the utmost utility as a collection of facts relative to later centuries, even though he does start with the assumption of the mark. But it is scarcely an answer to M. Fustel to argue, as Professor Lamprecht does,[1] that nothing depends on the *word* "mark;" and that the chance absence of a modern technical term from our meagre evidence does not prove the non-existence of the thing it is used to designate. For our evidence is not meagre; and M. Fustel proves not only the absence of the name, but also the absence of all the alleged indications of the existence of the thing.

The second line of defence is the evidence of "comparative custom." India, at any rate, it is urged, displays the village community: there we may see, crystallised by the force of custom, conditions which in Europe have long since passed away. Now it is, of course, true that the village is "the unit of all revenue arrangements in India;"[2] that, over large districts, cultivation is carried on by village groups; and that in some provinces, notably the Punjab, this village group is at present recognised as the joint owner of the village lands. But it is a long step from this to the proposition that "the oldest discoverable forms of property in land," in India, "were forms of collective property;"[3] and that all existing rights of private

---

[1] *Le Moyen Age* for June, 1889, p. 131.

[2] Sir George Campbell in *Tenure of Land in India*, one of the essays in *Systems of Land Tenure* (Cobden Club).

[3] Maine, *Village Communities*, p. 78; *Ancient Law*, p. 252.

ownership have arisen from the break-up or depres-
sion of the original communities. The truth is, that
of late years Indian facts have been looked at almost
exclusively through the spectacles of European theory.
Now that the mark is receding into improbability, it is
urgently to be desired that Indian economic history
should be looked at for what it will itself reveal.[1]   It
would be unwise to anticipate the results of such an
investigation. But there is one preliminary caution
to be expressed ; we must take care not to exaggerate
the force of custom. Professor Marshall, in his recent
great work, has indicated some of the reasons for believing that custom is by no means so strong in India
as is generally supposed ;[2] and it is to be hoped that
he will see his way to publishing the not-inconsider-
able mass of evidence that he has accumulated.

As to supposed analogies with the mark in the
practices of other peoples, all that can be said
at this stage is that most of them prove only a
joint-cultivation and not a joint-ownership. Thus,
the Russian *mir*, which is often referred to in this
connection, has always in historical times been a
village group in serfdom under a lord : the decree of
Boris Godounoff, frequently spoken of as the origin of
serfdom, in that it tied the cultivators to the soil,
may much more readily be explained as an attempt
to hinder a movement towards freedom. It was

[1] .... to A.   [2] *Principles of Economics*, p. 682, n.

indeed in all probability a measure somewhat similar
in character to the English "statutes of labourers".[1]
With regard to the various more or less savage peoples,
who are said to live under a system of common
village ownership, the bulk of the evidence is, as M.
Fustel observes, of the most unsubstantial character.
There are lessons in the work of M. Emile de Laveleye
which M. Fustel fails to recognise; and to these
we shall return; but to the main proposition
which it was intended to prove, M. de Laveleye's book can hardly be regarded as adding much
strength.

We see, then, that there is no very adequate reason,
either in German, Indian, Russian, or any other supposed analogies, why we should not suffer ourselves
to be guided in our judgment as to England by English
evidence. And this evidence, as we have seen, would
lead us to the conclusion that very soon after the
English Conquest, if not before, the manor was the
prevailing type of social organisation. The further
question still remains, what was its origin? This is a
question which cannot as yet be answered with certainty: but we are able to point out the possible
alternatives. For this purpose we must look for
a moment at each of the peoples that have succeed

---

[1] An account of it will be found in Faucher's essay on *Roman*
in Systems of Land Tenure; compare the English *statute of*
1388 in St. of the Realm, ii. 56. See Note D.

sively occupied England. Fortunately, there is no
need to go back to the very beginning, to the palæo-
lithic inhabitants of Britain who dwelt in the caves
and along the river-shores. Scanty in number, they
were extirpated by the more numerous and warlike
race that followed ; very much as the Esquimaux,
the kinsfolk, as it would seem, of prehistoric cave-men,
are being harried out of existence by the North
American Indians. There seems no reason to suppose
that these people contributed in any measure to the
formation of the later population of England.[1] But
with the race that took their place, a race of small
stature and long heads, the case is different. Ethno-
logists have long been of opinion that these pre-
Aryans were to a large extent the ancestors of the
present inhabitants of Western Europe ; and they
have of late won over to their side a rising school of
philologers,[2] some of whom go so far as to explain the
whole of modern history as the outcome of a struggle
between a non-Aryan populace and a haughty Aryan
aristocracy.[3] Without admitting any such hazardous
deductions, we may accept the statement that the blood
of these pre-Aryan people—*Iberians*, as it has become
usual to call them—is largely represented in the

[1] Boyd Dawkins, *Early Man in Britain*, p. 242.
[2] See the summary of recent philological discussion in Isaac
Taylor, *Origin of the Aryans*.
[3] Prof. Rhŷs in *New Princeton Review* for Jan., 1888.

English nation of to-day. Mr. Gomme has accordingly hazarded the supposition that our later rural
organisation is in part derived from the Iberian race.
He maintains that the traces of "terrace-cultivation,"
which we come across here and there in England and
Scotland, point to a primitive Iberian hill-folk, whose
"agricultural system," in some unexplained way, "became incorporated with the agricultural system of
the," later Aryan, "village community."[1] His argument turns chiefly on certain alleged Indian parallels.
But even if his examples proved the point for
India, which is hardly the case, there is in Britain
certainly no evidence for Mr. Gomme's contention.
If the terrace-cultivation is to be assigned to a
prehistoric people, the archæological data would
apparently place it in the bronze period [2]—an age
long subsequent to the Celtic immigration. And it
will be seen from what we have to say of the Celtic
inhabitants at a much later period that it is hardly
worth while to dwell upon the possibilities connected
with their predecessors.

For, to judge from the account given by Cæsar[3]—
who had abundant opportunities of observation—the
Britons, at the time of his invasion, were still, except
in Kent, in the pastoral stage. After speaking of the

[1] *Village Community* (1890), p. 71.
[2] Wilson, *Prehistoric Annals of Scotland*, vol. i. p. 492.
[3] *De Bello Gallico*, v. 14.

inhabitants of Kent as far more civilised than the
rest, he goes on to say, " most of those in the interior
sow no corn, but live on flesh and milk." Even if
his statement is not to be taken literally, there is this
further reason for believing that the village community
was not in existence among the Britons, *viz.*, that it did
not appear in those parts of the British Isles of which
the Celts retained possession until after they became
subject to external influences at a much later date.
Neither in Wales, nor in the Highlands, nor in Ireland,
can we find the village community until modern times.[1]
There was, indeed, some agriculture even when the
life was most pastoral. This agriculture was carried
on upon the "open-field" plan. There was, moreover,
a large number of dependent cultivators. But there
was nothing like the village group as it was to be
found in mediæval England.

When, however, we pass to the three centuries and a
half of Roman rule, we can hardly help coming to the
conclusion that it was during that period that England
became an agricultural country ; nor is it easy to
avoid the further conclusion that the agricultural
system then established remained during and after
the barbarian invasions. Take first the evidence for
the extension of agriculture. Some thirty years
after Claudius first set about the conquest of Britain,
and but seventeen years after the suppression of the

---

[1] Seebohm, *V.C.* 187, 223.

rebellion of the southern tribes led by Boadicea, Agricola became proconsul of Britain. Now, it appears from the account given by his biographer, Tacitus, that even as early as this the Roman tribute was collected in the form of corn. But we may gather that the cultivation of corn was only gradually spreading over the country; for we are told that Agricola had to interfere to prevent extortionate practices on the part of the revenue officers, who were in the habit of forcing the provincials to buy corn at an exorbitant rate from the Government granaries, in order to make up the prescribed quantity.[1] We may conjecture that the extension of agriculture was itself largely owing to the pressure of the Roman administration. But to whatever it may have been due, before the Roman rule had come to an end Britain had become celebrated for its production of corn. On one occasion, A.D. 360, the Emperor Julian had as many as eight hundred vessels built to carry corn from Britain to the starving cities on the Rhine. But by whom was the corn grown? We can hardly doubt that it was raised in Britain, as in other Roman provinces, on great private estates, surrounding the *villas* of wealthy land-owners, and cultivated by dependants of various grades—*coloni*, freedmen, slaves. Remains of Roman villas are scattered all over the

[1] *Agricola,* Chap. xix., and see the note in the edition of Church and Brodribb.

southern counties of England,[1] far too closely adjacent
one to another to allow us to think of the life
of Britain as "mainly military," or to look upon
Britain as " a Roman Algeria."[2]   It would be absurd
to suppose that these villas were all the residences of
wealthy officers or of provincials who derived their
income from official emoluments.   We should be
justified, even if we had no direct information, in
supposing that the *villa* meant in Britain very much
what it meant in Gaul and elsewhere; but, as it
chances, a decree of Constantine of the year 319 does
actually mention *coloni* and *tributarii* as present in
England;[3] and both these terms indicate classes
which, whether technically free or not, were none
the less dependent on a lord and bound to the soil.
And we can readily see how such a class would grow
up.   Some of the *coloni* may, as in Italy, have originally been free leaseholders, who had fallen into arrears
in the payment of their rent.   But there is no necessity for such a supposition.   Among the Gauls, as
Cæsar tells us, the only classes held in honour were
the druids and the knights (equites).   " The people "
(plebes), he says, " are regarded in much the same
light as slaves, without any initiative or voice in
public affairs; and many of them are forced by debt,

---

[1] How thickly the villas were scattered over the country is
shown by Wright, *Celt, Roman and Saxon* (3rd ed.), pp. 227 *seq.*
[2] These are the phrases of Green, *Making of England*, pp. 6, 7.
[3] Quoted in Seebohm, 294 n. 3.

or the pressure of taxation, or even by violence, actually to become the slaves of the more powerful."[1] In all probability the Romans found "knights" and "people" in the same relative position in Britain; and, indeed, when the unconquered tribes of Ireland and Wales come within the ken of history we find among them a large class of servile cultivators below the free tribesmen.[2] Whatever may have happened to the "knights," the "people" would easily become serfs bound to the soil on the various villas. Then, again, it must be noticed that it was the constant policy of the Roman emperors to provide for the needs both of agriculture and of military service by transporting conquered barbarians to distant provinces, and settling them on vacant or uncultivated lands. M. Fustel de Coulanges in his *Recherches*[3] shows that these barbarians were by no means turned into peasant proprietors; they became tenants, bound to the soil, upon the imperial domains or the estates of great proprietors. Britain enjoyed its share of the fruits of this policy; for in the later part of the second century Antoninus sent to Britain a number of Marcomanni; a century later, Probus transported hither a number of Burgundians and Vandals; and Valentinian, still a century later,

---

[1] *De Bello Gallico*, vi. 13.

[2] For Ireland, see Skene, *Celtic Scotland*, iii. pp. 139-140, 145; for Wales, A. N. Palmer, *Hist. of Ancient Tenures in the Marches of North Wales* [1885], pp. 77, 80.

[3] Pp. 43 sq.

sent a tribe of the Alamanni.[1] There is, therefore, no difficulty in accounting for the growth of a population of prædial serfs during the period of Roman rule.

If, however, we suppose that Southern Britain was divided during the period of Roman rule into estates cultivated by dependent tenants and slaves, there is much that would lead us to believe that the Roman agricultural system was retained by the English conquerors; even though, in the present state of our knowledge, we cannot directly prove continuity. The first and most important consideration is this: the English manorial system was substantially, and, indeed, in most of its details, similar to that which prevailed during the Middle Ages in Northern France and Western Germany. But these Continental conditions —it has, I think, conclusively been proved—were the direct continuation of conditions that had prevailed under Roman rule.[2] The natural conclusion is that what is true of the Continent is true also of England. This conviction is confirmed by looking at two of the fundamental characteristics of the English manor. The distinction between land *in villenage* and land *in demesne*—the latter cultivated by the tenants of the former, but yet kept in the lord's hands —is to be found in the mediaeval manor, and in the

---

[1] References in Seebohm, pp. 283, 287.
[2] Fustel de Coulanges, *L'Alleu et le Domaine Rural* (1889), pp. 34, 207, 227 *seq.*

Roman villa.[1] It is not to be found either in the tribal system of Wales,—which we may look upon as indicating the condition to which the Celtic inhabitants of Britain might have arrived if left to themselves; nor in Tacitus' account of the ancient Germans, which probably furnishes us in general outline with a picture of the social organisation which the English brought with them. Both in Wales and among the ancient Germans there were slaves working in their masters' houses, or on their farms, and there were also servile tenants paying dues in kind; but in neither case was there an obligation on the part of a tenant to labour on any other land than his own holding.

Another feature of the English manor was the division of its arable lands into three fields, with a regular rotation of crops, and with one field out of the three always fallow. Occasionally only two fields are to be found, sometimes as many as four; but by far the most usual number was three[2] Now it is a very significant fact that the three-field system has never been at all general in North-Western Germany, or in Jutland, the regions from which the English undoubtedly came; and it is for this reason that Professor Hanssen—who has given his

[1] *Ibid,* pp. 80 seq.
[2] This was pointed out, in correction of Rogers, by Nasse, *Agric. Community of M. A.,* pp. 52 seq.

whole life to the study of the agrarian history of Germany, and who is certainly not biassed by any antipathy to the mark theory — declares that the English cannot have brought the three-field system with them to Britain. Two hypotheses are tenable: either that it grew up in later centuries to meet the special needs of the country; or that it was found there when the English came. That this latter hypothesis is most probable would seem to be indicated by the fact that the region in Germany where it has been most widely prevalent is precisely that which was most Romanised, *viz.*, the South West.[1] We need not follow Mr. Seebohm in his ingenious attempt to show how it grew up in Southern Germany; it is sufficient for our present purpose to point out that the fact, however it may be explained, strengthens the probability that Roman influence had a good deal to do, in Britain also, with the creation of the conditions which we find in after times.

There are, therefore, many reasons for maintaining the permanence in Britain of the *villa* organisation; and we have seen above that while there are no clear traces of the *free* community, there are traces of what is afterwards called the manor, within a couple of centuries after the English conquest. These two lines of argument converge toward the conclusion that

---

[1] The bearing of these facts was first pointed out by Mr. Seebohm, *V.C.* pp. 372-4.

the manorial system dates in the main from the
period of Roman rule. But this conclusion does
not absolutely determine the other question, which
has been so warmly debated, as to the race to
which we are to assign the mass of the later population. It is expedient to narrow our inquiry to
the southern and midland shires of England, leaving out of consideration not only Wales, but also
the south-western peninsula, in which there is undoubtedly a preponderance of Celtic blood, and those
eastern and northern counties in which there was a
considerable Danish settlement. When we have solved
the main problem, it will be early enough to consider
these lesser difficulties. Unfortunately, even on the
main problem there is much to be done before we
can venture on a positive answer; and there need be
no haste to come to a decision. For the economic
historian the question is one of subordinate importance.
If he is allowed to take for his starting point, as the
result of recent discussion, that English social history
began with (1) the manor, (2) a population of dependent cultivators, it matters but little to him
what may have been the origin of the population.
The present position of the question may, however,
be stated in some such way as this. We can
hardly suppose a continuity in system unless a considerable number of the old cultivators were left to
work it. The reasonableness of such a supposition

has been obscured by its unfortunate association by certain writers with the wild idea that the whole fabric of Roman society and political machinery survived the English conquest. There is absolutely no good evidence for such a survival; and Mr. Freeman has justly pointed out[1] that, had it been the case, the subsequent history of Britain would have resembled that of Gaul, instead of forming a marked contrast to it. But the disappearance of the Roman political organisation, and the destruction on the battlefield of Roman or Romanised land-*owners*, is not inconsistent with the undisturbed residence upon the rural estates of the great body of actual labourers. The English had been far less touched by Roman civilisation than the Franks; they met with a resistance incomparably more determined than that offered by the Provincials to the barbarians in any other part of the empire; and they remained Pagan for more than a century after the invasion. These facts sufficiently explain the savagery which distinguished the English from the Frankish invasion. But however terrible the English may have been in their onslaught, it was obviously for their interest, while taking the place of the landlords, to avail themselves of the labour of the existing body of labourers. And if the Roman upper class was killed out in England and not in Gaul, this would furnish a fairly adequate

---

[1] Most recently in *Four Oxford Lectures* (1887), pp. 61 *seq.*

explanation of the fact that in Gaul the language of
the conquered is spoken, and in England that of the
conquerors.

It is reassuring to find, on referring to Gibbon's chapter on the English conquest of Britain, that this conclusion agrees with the judgment of one " whose lightest
words are weighty."[1]   Gibbon dwells as strongly as
anyone could wish on the thorough character of the
English operations: "Conquest has never appeared more
dreadful or destructive than in the hands of the Saxons."
He lays due stress on the fate of Andredes-Ceaster: "the
last of the Britons, without distinction of age or sex,
was massacred in the ruins of Anderida; and the
repetition of such calamities was frequent and familiar
under the Saxon heptarchy."   He asserts, with vigorous rhetoric, that a clean sweep was made of the
Roman administrative organisation :

> " The arts and religion, the laws and language, which the
> Romans had so carefully planted in Britain, were extirpated by
> their barbarous successors. . . The kings of France maintained
> the privileges of their Roman subjects, but the ferocious Saxons
> trampled on the laws of Rome and of the emperors. The pro-
> ceedings of civil and criminal jurisdiction, the titles of honour,
> the forms of office, the ranks of society . . . were finally sup-
> pressed. . . The example of a revolution, so rapid and so com-
> plete, may not easily be found."

Nevertheless, he does not agree with those who hold
that such a revolution involved either the " extirpa-

[1] Freeman, *Norman Conquest*, vol. v. ch. xxiv. p. 334.

tion " or the " extermination " or even the " displace-
ment " of the subject population.

> " This strange alteration has persuaded historians, *and even philosophers*" (an amusing touch) " that the provincials of Britain were totally exterminated ; and that the vacant land was again peopled by the perpetual influx and rapid increase of the German colonies. . . . But neither reason nor facts can justify the unnatural supposition that the Saxons of Britain remained alone in the desert which they had subdued. After the sanguinary barbarians had secured their dominion, and gratified their revenge, *it was their interest to preserve the peasants as well as the cattle* of the unresisting country. In each successive revolution the patient herd becomes the property of its new masters ; and the salutary compact of food and labour is silently ratified by their mutual necessities."[1]

A weightier argument than that of language has been based on the history of religion. Little import-ance, indeed, can be attached to the fact that in Gaul there was no break in the episcopate or in the diocesan system, while in England both needed to be re-established by Augustine and Theodore. For even if the diocesan system had existed in Britain before the English invasion—which is doubtful[2]—it would dis-appear with the destruction of the governing classes. It is a more important consideration that if Britain had been thoroughly Christianised, and if a large Christian population had continued to dwell in the country, we should surely have had some reference to these native Christians in the accounts we subsequently

---

[1] *Decline and Fall*, ch. xxxviii.
[2] See Hatch, *Growth of Church Institutions*, pp. 15, 39.

obtain of the conversion of the English. But we know
very little of British Christianity; it might have been
strong in the cities, and even among the gentry in the
country, without having any real hold upon the rural
population—the *pagani* as they were called elsewhere.
Dr. Hatch, speaking of the condition of Gaul when
the Teutonic invasions began, has told us that the mass
of the Celtic peasantry was still unconverted.[1] And
this is still more likely to be true of Britain. Even if
nominally Christian, half-heathen serfs, left without
churches or priests, would soon relapse into paganism;
especially as it would be their interest to accept the
religion of their conquerors. The exact force of the
argument as to religion must be left as undetermined.

There is another source of information to which we
might naturally turn, considering how much has been
heard of it of late years. We might expect some
assistance from "craniology:" the character of the
skulls found in interments of the period of the English
settlement ought to tell something as to the races to
which they belonged. But although much attention
has been given to pre-historic barrows, there has
been comparatively little scientific examination of
cemeteries of a later date. There are, at present,
not enough ascertained facts to speak for themselves; and such facts as have been gathered have
usually been interpreted in the light of some parti-

[1] *Ibid.* p. 10.

cular theory. When we find the late Professor Rolleston telling us that there are as many as five distinct types of skull belonging to inhabitants of Britain just before the English invasion, as well as two separate types of English skulls,[1] we see how wide a room there is for conjecture. Yet from his careful investigation of a Berkshire cemetery, which was probably characteristic of mid-England as a whole, there are two results on which we may venture to lay stress. One is that such evidence as it furnishes runs counter to the theory of intermarriage,[2] which has been so frequently resorted to in order to temper the severity of the pure Teutonic doctrine. This is intelligible enough. If the mass of the lower people were allowed to remain, while the place of the upper classes was taken by the English invaders, intermarriage would seldom take place. The other is that there are abundant relics, among the English graves, of a long-headed race, which can fairly be identified with the Iberian type as modified by increasing civilisation ; and but scanty relics of the broad-headed Celt.[3] This fits in very readily with the supposition that under the Celtic, and therefore under the Roman rule, the cultivating class was largely composed of the pre-Celtic race ; and allows

[1] *Archæologia* xlii. espec. pp. 464-465.

[2] *Ibid.* p. 459.

[3] *Ibid.* 464.   Cf. for traces of Iberians in other districts, Greenwell and Rolleston, *British Barrows*, p. 679.

us to believe that the agricultural population was but little disturbed.

But though the cultivators already at work were probably left as they were, it is very likely that they were joined by many new-comers. We can hardly suppose that *free* English warriors would have settled down at once as tillers of the soil, toiling half the days of the week on land not their own. But Tacitus describes a class of persons among the Germans whom he repeatedly calls *slaves*, and speaks of as subject to the arbitrary authority of their masters. They were not, he expressly says, employed in gangs, as on a Roman villa; but each man had his own house and family, and rendered to his master no other service than the periodical payment of a certain quantity of corn, or cattle, or cloth. He goes so far as to compare this class with the Roman *coloni*, though they differed from them in not being *legally* free. He calls our attention further to the presence of a number of *freedmen*, occupying a position but little above that of slaves. There is no reason at all to suppose that Tacitus regarded these slaves and freedmen as few in number. And if there were slaves and freedmen in the same position among the invading English, they would readily fall into the ranks of the servile cultivators.[1]

[1] *Germania*, cc. 24, 25 ; and see the commentary of Fustel de Coulanges in *Recherches*, pp. 205-211.

On the whole, we may conclude that the main features of the later manorial system were of Roman origin, and that a large part—how large we are unable to say—of the working population was of Provincial blood. But it does not follow that every later manor represents a Roman villa, or that all the Roman estates had the extent of the manors which now represent them. In both of these directions there was opportunity for much later development: many new manors were doubtless created on new clearings, and many old manors were enlarged. It would be easy enough to create fresh servile tenancies if there was a large body of slaves; and such there certainly was even in the early centuries of the English occupation. One of the most unfortunate consequences of the mark theory has been to create a vague impression that any condition lower than absolute freedom was altogether exceptional in early English society. But we can hardly turn over the old English laws without seeing that this could not have been the case. Not only is there frequent reference to slaves, but manumission occupies as prominent a position as in the Continental codes, was accomplished by ceremonies of a similar character, and brought with it the same consequence in the abiding subjection of the freedman to his former master.[1] As

[1] The passages relating to the subject are brought together in a volume of old-fashioned learning—*A Dissertation upon Distinctions in Society and Ranks of the People under the Anglo-*

on the Continent also, the Church interfered for the
slave's protection, and endeavoured to secure for
him a property in the fruits of his labour.[1] It is not
necessary to revert to the discussion as whence this
class came. It is enough to point to it as explaining
the extension of the manorial system. It will, however, be noticed that every fresh proof that the conditions of society in England were similar to those
on the Continent strengthens the argument of the
preceding pages.

There is one further element in the problem which
must not be overlooked. Mr. Seebohm's doctrine that
the later villeins were descended from servile dependants has perhaps led some to suppose that the only
alternative to the mark theory is the supposition
that the villeins of the Middle Ages were all the
descendants of slaves. But here the analogy of
Continental conditions is again of use. Though
there is no trace of the free village community,
at any rate in historical times, and the villa with
its slaves was the germ of the later seigneury; yet
the servile tenants of subsequent centuries were to no
small extent the descendants of *coloni*, who, though

Saxon Governments, by Samuel Heywood [1818], pp. 317 seq,
413 seq. Cf. Fustel de Coulanges, *L'Alleu*, chaps. x., xi.

[1] *Penitential* of Theodore [xix. 20, in Thorpe, *Ancient Laws
and Institutes*, p. 286 ; xiii. 3, in Haddon and Stubbs, *Chronicle*
iii. p. 202]. *Penitential* of Egbert [Addit. 36, in Thorpe,
p. 391.]

bound to the soil, were still technically free, centuries
after the Roman rule had passed away.[1] And so in
the early English laws we find men technically free,
whom, none the less, it can scarcely be exaggeration
to describe as *serfs.* Such, for instance, is the freeman who works on the Sabbath "by his lord's command,"[2] or who kills a man "by his lord's command;"[3]
who pays a fine if he goes from his lord without leave;[4]
or who receives from his lord a dwelling as well as
land, and so becomes bound not only to the payment
of rent, but also to the performance of labour services.[5]
Yet, the *colonus* of pre-English days and his descendants might long retain a position superior to that
of a slave with an allotment. In obscure differences
of this kind may possibly be found the origin of the
distinction between the "privileged" and "unprivil-
eged" villeins of later centuries.[6]

---

[1] Fustel de Coulanges, *L'Alleu*, pp. 359, 413. Such a use of
the term "free" may, perhaps, help to explain the phrase with
regard to the *cotsetla* in the *Rectitudines:* "Det super heorth-
penig. . . . *sicut omnis liber facere debet*" ("*eal swá erlean frigean
men gebyreth*"). Thorpe, p. 185.

[2] Thorpe, *Ancient Laws*, p. 45 (Ine, 3).

[3] *Ibid.* 316 (Theodore).

[4] *Ibid.* 55 (Ine, 39).

[5] *Ibid.* 63 (Ine, 67).

[6] As stated, for instance, in Britton, ed. Nicholls, ii., p. 13.
Privileged villeins were, it is true, only to be found on the royal
demesnes. But in the later Roman empire, the *Coloni* upon
the imperial estates were an especially numerous and important
class. (Fustel de Coulanges, *Recherches*, pp. 28-32). That there

It must be allowed that there is still very much that is obscure in the early history of villeinage. This obscurity may be expected to disappear as social antiquities come to be studied by scholars who are economists as well as historians. It was on the economic side, if the criticism may be ventured, that M. Fustel de Coulanges was weak. He never seemed to grasp the difference between what we may call the joint-husbandry of the mediæval village group, and the liberty of the modern farmer to make of his land what he pleases. While pointing out that M. de Laveleye does not prove common *ownership*, he fails to realise that, even if this is so, the joint-husbandry, with its appurtenant common rights, is a phenomenon of the utmost interest, and deserves careful attention. He seems to think that it explains itself; although, the more complex and the more widespread it proves to be, the less likely does it seem that it originated in the miscellaneous promptings of individual self-interest.

We may perhaps state the problem thus. In the mediæval manor there were two elements, the *seigneurial*—the relations of the tenants to the lord; and the *communal*—the relations of the tenants to one

another. The mark theory taught that the seigneurial was grafted on to the communal. The value of
the work of M. Fustel de Coulanges and of Mr. Seebohm
is in showing that we cannot find a time when the
seigneurial element was absent; and also in pointing
to reasons, in my opinion conclusive, for connecting
that element with the Roman villa. But the communal element is still an unsolved mystery. Among
the difficulties which lie on the surface in M.
Fustel's treatment of the question, it may be worth
while to mention two. He insists that the *villa*
itself, from the earliest time at which it appears,
has a unity which it retains throughout.[1] This
seems to suggest some earlier economic formation
out of which it arose; for if the villas were originally
nothing more than private estates, like the estates
formed in a new country in our own day, they would
hardly have had such a fixity of outline. Then, again,
nothing is more characteristic of the later manor than
the *week-works*, the labour performed by each villien
for two or three days every week on the lord's
demesne. But such week-works do not appear in
mediæval documents until A.D. 622.[2] M. Fustel
hardly realises that a fact like this requires explana-

---

[1] *L'Alleu*, pp. 20-21.

[2] *Leges Alamannorum* qu. Seebohm, p. 323. It is, however,
possible that the "*binae aratoriae*," etc., on the *Saltus Buritanus*
meant more than two *days*, although that is the interpretation
of M. Fustel de Coulanges. See *Recherches*, p. 33.

tion; or, indeed, that such services were far more onerous than any he describes in the case of the earlier *coloni*.

Difficulties such as these can only be satisfactorily overcome by taking into account both sides of the subject—the economic as well as the constitutional or legal. Side by side with a development which combined together gangs of slaves and the households of dependent coloni into the homogeneous class of serfs, and then went on to make out of the mediæval serf the modern freeman, another series of changes was going on of which M. Fustel de Coulanges says nothing. It was the development from a " wild field grass husbandry," where a different part of the area in occupation was broken up for cultivation from time to time, to the "three-field system " with its permanent arable land pasture, and then again from that to the " convertible husbandry " and the "rotation of crops " of more recent times. The task for the economic historian is to put these two developments into their due relation the one to the other.

The study of economic history is altogether indispensable, if we are ever to have anything more than a superficial conception of the evolution of society. But it must be thorough ; and we must not be overhasty in proclaiming large results. And although a principal motive for such inquiry will be the hope of obtaining some light on the direction in which change is likely to take place in the future, it will be wise for some time to come for students resolutely to turn away their eyes from current controversies. There is a sufficient lesson in the topic we have been considering. The history of the mark has served Mr. George as a basis for the contention that the common ownership of land is the only natural condition of things; to Sir Henry Maine it has suggested the precisely opposite conclusion that the whole movement of civilisation has been from common ownership to private. Such arguments are alike worthless, if the mark never existed.

NOTE A.—ON THE VILLAGE IN INDIA.

It has been remarked above that the history of land-tenure in India calls for fresh examination, unbiassed by any theory as to its development in Europe. It may, however, be added that, so far as may be judged from the material already accessible to us, India supports the mark-hypothesis as little as England. The negative argument may be thus drawn out :—1. The village-groups under the Mogul empire were bodies of cultivators with a customary right of occupation. The proprietor of the soil, in theory and in practice, was the Great Mogul. The dispute between the two schools of English officials early in the present century as to whether the *ryot* could properly be regarded as an owner or not, arose from an attempt to make Indian facts harmonise with English conceptions. The *ryot* had, indeed, a fixity of tenure greater than that of an ordinary English tenant; on the other hand, the share of the produce which he was bound to pay to the emperor or his delegate " amounted to a customary rent, raised to the highest point to which it could be raised without causing the people to emigrate or rebel " (Sir George Campbell, in *Systems of Land Tenure*). The French traveller, Bernier,

who resided in India twelve years, and acted as physician to
Aurungzebe, describes in 1670 the oppression to which the
"peasantry" were subjected, and discusses the question
"whether it would not be more advantageous for the king as
well as for the people, if the former ceased to be sole possessor
of the land, and the right of private property were recognised
in India as it is with us" (*Travels*, tr. Brock, i., p. 255).

2. Can we get behind the period of Mugul rule, and discover
whether it was super-imposed directly on a number of free cultivating groups, or whether it swept away a class of landlords?
Such an opportunity seems to be presented by the institutions
of Rajputana, which are described by Sir Alfred Lyall as "the
only ancient political institutions now surviving upon any considerable scale in India," and as having suffered little essential
change between the eleventh and nineteenth centuries (*Asiatic
Studies*, pp. 185, 193). "In the Western Rajput States the
conquering clans are still very much in the position which they
took up on first entry upon the lands. They have not driven
out, slain, or absolutely enslaved the anterior occupants, or
divided off the soil among groups of their own cultivating
families . . . . Their system of settlement was rather that of
the Gothic tribes after their invasion of the Danubian provinces
of the Roman empire, who, according to Finlay, 'never formed
the bulk of the population in the lands which they occupied, but
were only lords of the soil, principally occupied in war and
hunting.' In a Rajput State of the best preserved original type,
we still find all the territory . . . . . partitioned out among the
Rajputs, in whose hands is the whole political and military
organisation. . . . . . . Under the Rajputs are the cultivating
classes . . . . who now pay land rent to the lords or their families,
living in village communities with very few rights and privileges,
and being too often no more than rack-rented peasantry" (*Ibid.*,
p. 197). Here, it is true, we have a case of conquest by an
invading race; but if this be compared with the description
given by Sir William Hunter of the constitution of Orissa under

d

its native princes, before the period of Mahometan rule, it will
be seen that the condition of the cultivators was much the same,
whoever might be their masters. Orissa would seem to have
been d vided into two parts, the royal domain "treated as a
private estate and vigilantly administered by means of land-
bailiffs," and the estates of the "feudal nobility," known as
Fort-holders (*Orissa*, pp. 214-219).   In the petty Tributary
States in the neighbourhood of British Orissa, there are said to
be now no intermediary holders between the husbandman and
the Rajah, "in whom rests the abstract ownership, while the
right of occupancy remains with the actual cultivator." The
condition of things reproduces, therefore, on a small scale and
subject to British control, what was to be found on an immensely
larger scale under the Mogul emperors. Whether there ever
were in these districts lords of land between the prince and the
peasant is not clear.   •

3. Sir William Hunter suggests that we can distinguish an
even earlier stage. "We know," he says (p. 206), "that the
Aryan invaders never penetrated in sufficient numbers into India
to engross any large proportion of the soil. That throughout
five-sixths of the continent, the actual work of tillage remained
in the hands of the Non-Aryan or Sudra races ; and that, even
at a very remote time, husbandry had become a degrading
occupation in the eyes of the Aryan conquerors. . . . . In
Orissa, where Aryan colonisation never amounted to more than
a thin top-dressing of priests and *nobles*, the generic word of
husbandman is sometimes used as a synonym for the Non-Aryan
caste. At this day, we see the acknowledged aboriginal castes
of the mountains in the very act of passing into the low-caste
cultivators of the Hindu village, as soon as Hindu civilisation
penetrates their glens." He thinks it probable, therefore, that
the Hindu village is the "outcome" of Non-Aryan Hamlets
such as those of the Kandhs. This is not unlikely ; but supposing the conjecture to be correct, we must notice two essential
points. The first is that the Kandh Hamlet, with its popula-

them of, on an average, some five-and-thirty persons, is nothing
more than a cluster of independent households, placed close
together for mutual protection. The absolute ownership of the
soil is vested in each family; and the Hamlet as a whole
exercises no corporate authority whatever (pp. 72, 77, 209, 210).
And in the second place, if the Hamlet expanded into the
village and the village became that "firmly cohering entity"
which it now is, land-lordship would seem to have developed
pari passu (*Ibid*, pp. 212-3). At no stage of agrarian history do
we find the village community of theory, which is "an *organised
self-acting* group of families exercising a *common proprietorship*
over a definite tract of land*" (Maine, *Village Communities*, pp.
10, 12). Where the cultivating group are in any real sense proprietors, they have no corporate character; and where they have
a corporate character, they are not proprietors.

NOTE B.—ON THE RUSSIAN MIR.

Since the preceding chapter was written, fresh light has been
cast on the history of the Russian village group by the work of
M. Kovalevsky, *Modern Customs and Ancient Laws of Russia*
(London, 1891). According to M. Kovalevsky, the view that
the peasants retained their personal liberty until the decrees of
Boris Godounoff at the end of the sixteenth century deprived
them of freedom of migration, is now generally abandoned by
Russian scholars (pp. 210-211); and it is recognised that long
before that date serfdom of a character similar to that of western
Europe was in existence, over, at any rate, a considerable area
of the Empire. Still more significant is another fact on which
M. Kovalevsky lays great stress. It is commonly asserted, or
implied, that the custom of periodical re-division of the lands
of the mir is a survival from ancient usage, and forms a transi-
tional stage between common and individual ownership (e.g.,
Maine, *Ancient Law*, pp. 267-270). But M. Kovalevsky assures
us that the practice is quite modern; that it dates no further

back than last century; and that it was due chiefly to Peter the
Great's imposition of a capitation tax (pp. 93-97).

M. Kovalevsky is none the less a strenuous supporter of the
village community theory; and he is indignant with M. Fustel
for "endorsing an opinion," that of M. Tchitcherin, "which
has already been refuted" by M. Beliaiev. Unfortunately he
does not cite any of the facts on which M. Beliaiev relied. He
himself allows that but scanty evidence can be found in old
Russian documents in support of the theory (pp. 74, 82); and
bases his own argument rather on what has taken place in recent
centuries, from the sixteenth down to our own day, when out-
lying territories have been colonized by immigrants. But this
is a dangerous method of proof when used by itself; it would
lead, for instance, to the conclusion that because the early communities in New England were not subject to manorial lords,
there had never been manorial lords in England. And even in
the cases he describes, "the unlimited right of private home-
steads to appropriate as much soil as each required was scrupulously maintained" (p. 80)—which is very different from the
Mark of Maurer.

THE ORIGIN OF PROPERTY IN LAND.

During the last forty years a theory has made its way into historical literature, according to which private ownership in land was preceded by a system of cultivation in common. The authors of this theory do not confine themselves to saying that there was no such thing as private property in land among mankind when in a primitive or savage state. It is obvious that when men were still in the hunting or pastoral stage, and had not yet arrived at the idea of agriculture, it did not occur to them to take each for himself a share of the land. The theory of which I speak applies to settled and agricultural societies. It asserts that among peoples that had got so far as to till the soil in an orderly fashion, common ownership of land was still maintained; that for a long time it never occurred to these men who ploughed, sowed, reaped and planted, to appropriate to themselves the ground upon which they laboured. They only looked upon it as belonging to the community. It was the people that

A

at first was the sole owner of the entire territory, either cultivating it in common, or making a fresh division of it every year. It was only later that the right of property, which was at first attached to the whole people, came to be associated with the village, the family, the individual.

"All land in the beginning was common land," says Maurer, "and belonged to all; that is to say to the people."[1] "Land was held in common," says M. Viollet, "before it became private property in the hands of a family or an individual."[2] "The arable land was cultivated in common," says M. de Laveleye; "private property grew up afterwards out of this ancient common ownership."[3] In a word, the system of agriculture was, in the beginning, an agrarian communism.

This theory is not, strictly speaking, a new one. Long before the present century, there were thinkers who loved to picture to themselves mankind living together, when society was first formed, in a fraternal communism. What is new in this, what is peculiar to our own times, is the attempt to rest this theory on a foundation of historical fact, to support it with quota-

[1] G. L. von Maurer, *Einleitung zur Geschichte der Mark- Hof- Dorf- und Stadtverfassung,* 1854, p. 93.

[2] P. Viollet, in the *Bibliothèque de l' Ecole des Chartes,* 1872, p. 503.

[3] Em. de. Laveleye, *De la propriété et de ses formes primitives,* 1874.

tions from historical documents, to deck it out, so to speak, in a learned dress.

I do not wish to combat the theory. What I want to do is only to examine the authorities on which it has been based. I intend simply to take *all* these authorities, as they are presented to us by the authors of the system, and to verify them. The object of this cold and tedious procedure is not that of proving whether the theory is true or false; it is only to discover whether the authorities that have been quoted can be fairly regarded as appropriate. In short, I am going to discuss not the theory itself, but the garb of learning in which it has been presented.

I.

The theory of Maurer as to community of land amongst the Germanic nations.

G. L. von Maurer is, if not the earliest, at any rate the chief author of the theory we are examining.

He presented it with great clearness in a book published in 1854. In this he maintained that, amongst the Germans, private domains, villages and towns, all spring alike from a primitive *mark*; that this primitive mark consisted of an area of land held in common; that the land was cultivated for a long period without there being any private property; and that the cultivators formed amongst themselves an " association of

the mark," a "*markgenossenschaft.*" "All land," he
said, " was in the beginning common-land, *gemeinland*
or *allmende*" (page 93). "There was nothing which
could be rightly termed private property" *(ibid)*.
"The ground was divided into equal lots, and this
division was made afresh each year; every member
received a part and moved each year to a new lot."
"The whole mark, cultivated land as well as forests,
was held in common " (p. 97).

" The idea of property," he says again, "only came
as a result of Roman law " (p. 103). " Property, as
we find it in later times, was produced by the decom-
position of the ancient mark " (p. 10).

Our author re-stated his doctrine in another book
published two years later: " The associations of the
mark are bound up with the primitive cultivation of
the soil; they can be traced back to the earliest
German settlements, and in a¹¹ probability once
occupied the whole of Germany."[1] We have to
consider what are the facts, and what the authorities
on which Maurer builds up this doctrine.

As the question concerns very early times, he
naturally begins with early authorities. The first is
Cæsar. Cæsar calls our attention, we are told, to the

---

[1] *Geschichte der Markverfassung*, 1856. The same theory has
been reproduced with slight differences, and sometimes fresh
exaggerations by Waitz, *Deutsche Verfassungsgeschichte*, 3 edit.,
I., pp. 125-131 ; Sohm, *Reichs- und Gerichtsverfassung*, pp. 117,
209-210.

fact that amongst the Germans " there are no separate estates or private boundaries." [1]

This is explicit; and, although one might say that Cæsar was unacquainted with the Germans at home,[2] it has great weight as coming from so clear-headed a writer. Let me, however, call attention to the fact that the passage from Cæsar is by no means a description of the mark as Maurer and his disciples conceive it. Cæsar does not show us a *markgenossenschaft*, an association of peasants cultivating in common land of which they were the common owners. He describes, and this is a very different thing, the chiefs of the cantons arbitrarily disposing of the soil of which they alone appear to be the owners, and each year moving families and groups of men from one place to another. These people apparently have no rights, no power of initiative; the chiefs leave them only " as much land as they think fit," " where they think fit," and they " force them " to move from place to place. All this is far enough removed from the supposed association of the mark—an association, that is, of free peasants cultivating land in common, in virtue of their joint ownership; and it would be difficult to make Cæsar's observation fit into such a condition of things.[3]

[1] Cæsar, vi., 22.

[2] The expedition upon the right bank of the Rhine lasted only 18 days.

[3] *Neque quisquam agri modum certum aut fines habet proprios ; et magistratus ac principes in annos singulos gentibus cognationibus-*

Next comes Tacitus. Does he introduce the mark
into the picture which he draws of the institutions of
the Germans? "Yes," says Maurer; "for in his
26th chapter, when he uses the word *agri* he means
the mark." And again, "all land held in common
and not divided, Tacitus calls *ager*." But by what
authority does Maurer translate *agri* in Tacitus, and
further on *ager*, by "common lands," when the word
common is not to be found there? "Because," says he,
"the word *ager*, in the Roman sense, signified when used
by itself *ager publicus*." Here we have an apparently
unimportant philological statement, but it is one
which plays a considerable part in Maurer's book.
He repeats it three times (pages 6, 84, and 93). Indeed, if we look more closely into it, we find that it is
the foundation of his system. It was necessary for
his view that the mark should be found in Tacitus;
and therefore the word *ager* by itself had to mean
ager publicus, i.e., mark, common land, *Gemeinland.*
This is exactly what has to be proved. The true
sense of a word cannot be got at by an effort of
imagination, or by turning over the pages of a pocket-
dictionary. It is only to be found by bringing together
a number of examples of its use and comparing
them; and the term *ager* occurs so often in Latin
literature that an attentive student can hardly make

*busque hominum qui una coierunt, quantum et quo loco visum est,
agri attribuunt, atque anno post alio transire cogunt.*

any mistake as to its meaning. Nowhere do we find
it in the sense of public land, unless when accompanied
by the adjective *publicus* or the genitive *populi*, or
some other term to show clearly the especial meaning
it is intended to have.[1] By itself it never meant
public land. Read Cato and Varro; they do not once
mention public lands; and yet the word *ager* occurs
frequently in their works, each time in the sense of a
private estate. Some one buys an *ager*; the owner
makes the lustration of his *ager* (Cato, 141), that is to
say, he perambulates the boundaries of his property.

[1] Livy has been cited; but if those who have done so had
first read him, they would have seen that every time that he
wishes to speak of public land, he says *ager publicus* and not
ager by itself. ii. 41 : agrum publicum possideri a privatis
criminabatur. ii. 61 : Possessores agri publici. iv. 36 : agris
publicis. iv. 51 : possesso per injuriam agro publico. iv. 53 :
possessione agri publici coderent. vi. 5 : in possessione agri
publici grassabantur, etc. That it sometimes happens that in a
passage where he has written *ager publicus*, he afterwards writes
ager without the adjective, is natural enough. If he speaks in
one place of *triumverorum agro dividndo* or *de agris dividendis ploti*,
he has no need to add the adjective which is obviously understood. In chapter xxxv. of book vi. he speaks of the *lex
Licinia* " *de modo agrorum*," i.e., as to the maximum size of
rural properties. It has been conjectured that he made a mistake, and that he meant to speak of the *ager publicus*; but this
is very doubtful. Varro, *de re rustica* 1, 2, and Columella, 1, 3,
understand the law as Livy does; they see in it a limitation of
property in general. I cannot, therefore, agree with M.
d'Arbois de Jubainville, who interprets *de modo agrorum*, as if it
were *de modo agri publici*. We must translate literally, and not
change the sense.

Columella is continually talking about the *ager* as
the property of a man whom he calls *dominus*.
More than thirty passages in Cicero show that he
drew a distinction between an *ager*, which was the
property of a private citizen, and the *ager publicus*,
which was the property of the state. Even the
agrarian laws, whose real object was to transform an
ager publicus into an *ager privatus*, mark clearly the
difference between them.[1]

It is, therefore, in no sense true that the word *ager*
by itself implied public or common land, or that it
was in any way analogous to the word *mark*. So far
was this from being the case, that a Roman jurisconsult
expressly says that the dominant idea conveyed by
the word *ager* is that of complete ownership.[2]

In fact, what a Roman calls *ager* was very often
what we call an estate. In Cato, for instance, the

---

[1] See the *Lex dicta Thoria*, in the *Corpus inscriptionum latina-
rum*, I., p. 79 : " Qui ager publicus populi romani fuit . . . ager
privatus esto, ejusque agri emptio venditio uti ceterorum agrorum privatorum esto."

[2] Javolenus, in the *Digest*, 50, 16, 115 : " Possessio ab agro
juris proprietate distat ; quidquid enim adprehendimus cujus
proprietas ad nos non pertinet, hoc possessionem appellamus ;
possessio ergo usus, ager proprietas loci est." Notice that this
idea of property is found even in the expression *ager publicus*,
which does not at all mean common land ; it means the property
of the state, the public domain. If Maurer and his German or
French disciples had known Latin or Roman institutions a little
better, they would never have identified the *ager publicus* with
the *allmend*.

ager is not simply a field; it is a domain of some 60, 75, or 150 acres (c.c. 1, 10), which is cultivated by ten, twelve or sixteen slaves. Columella mentions, as if it were not unusual, that an *ager* might be so extensive that the owner would have to divide it for purposes of agriculture between several groups of slaves. *Ager* and *fundus* are synonymous terms, and they both mean an area of land cultivated for an owner's benefit.[1] Pliny speaks in his letters of his *agri*; and each of them is a great estate that he either lets out to farmers, or cultivates by means of a body of slaves. Each *ager* included, to judge from his description, arable land, meadows, vineyards and woods. The jurisconsult Paulus makes use of the two words, *ager* and *fundus*, in referring to one and the same domain.[2] Another jurisconsult says in so many words that the word *ager* includes all the land of an estate.[3] Finally, if there were still any doubt, we need only look at the passage from Ulpian in the *Digest*, which gives the formula under which estates were enrolled in the census. We see that such properties are called *agri*, and that each of them comprises land in tillage, vineyards, meadows, and forests.[4]

<hr>

[1] As to the synonymous character of these two words, see Varro, *De re rustica*, 1, 4, where both are used for the same thing, for another example, see *ibidem*, Iii. 2. Similarly Columella, 1, 2 and 1, 4, pp. 27 and 33 of the bipontine edition.

[2] Paul, in the *Digest*, xviii. 1, 40.

[3] *Digest*, L., 16, 211.

[4] Ulpian, in the *Digest*, L., 16, 4 : " Forma censuali cavetur

All this has to be borne in mind, if we would know what was the idea that Tacitus associated with the word *agri;* for no doubt Tacitus used the language of the Romans of his own times. To suppose that he attached to this word a meaning it had never had, *viz.*, *public* land, and, going even further, the idea of *common* land—an idea which never entered the Roman brain—is pure fancy. And this is the error with which Maurer and his followers set out to misinterpret the whole of chapter xxvi. of the Germania.[1]

ut agri sic in censum referantur : nomen fundi cujusque, arvum quot jugerum sit, vinea. . pratum,. . . pascua. . . silvæ."

[1] We have shown elsewhere (*Recherches sur quelques problèmes d'histoire*, pp. 269-289) the mistakes which have been committed as to the words *agri, occupantur, cultores, arva, mutant, superest ager.* On the special meaning of *occupare agrum*, to put land to account by placing slaves upon it, see Columella, ii. 9 ; ii. 10 ; ii. 11 ; ii. 13 ; v. 5 ; v. 10 ; notice especially these two passages, Columella, i. 3 : occupatos nexu civium aut ergastulis, and *Code* of Justinian, ix. 49, 7 : quot mancipia in prædiis occupatis teneantur. As to the meaning of *cultores*, we must remember the *coloni* of whom Tacitus has spoken in the previous chapter. For the meaning of *arva*, see Varro, *De re rustica*, i. 29 : arvum est quod aratum est; *ibid.*, i. 13 : boves ex arvo reducti; i. 19 : ad jugera ducenta arvi, boum jugo duo; cf. Cicero, *De republ.*, v. 2, and especially *Digest*, L., 15, 4. *Mutare* does not mean to exchange among themselves ; to express that meaning *inter se* would have been needed : *mutare* by itself is the frequentative of *movere*, and means to shift. The Germans shifted their tillage, and tilled now one part, now another of the estate. If we translate each of the words of Tacitus literally, especially if we pay attention to the context and read the entire chapter, *nec pomaria, nec hortos,* . . . . *sola seges,* etc., we see that Tacitus

After Tacitus, we have the early records of German law. Is this where Maurer discovers the mark ? If the system of the mark was in full vigour in early times, and came down from them to more modern days, proof of its existence would certainly be found in barbaric law. But the word *mark* is not to be met with in those codes. You find it neither in the laws of the Burgundians nor in those of the Visigoths, nor in those of the Lombards ; nor do you find any term that might be its equivalent or translation. It is absent, in like manner, from the Salic law.

In the Ripuarian law the *word* is to be found, but in a sense quite the opposite of that which Maurer attributes to it. Far from implying a district of land common to all, it denotes the boundary of a private estate. This will be seen on reading section 60 : " If any one buys a villa or any small estate, he ought to procure witnesses to the sale... If a proprietor encroaches on a neighbouring proprietor (this is the

---

is describing the method of cultivation among the Germans, and that it does not occur to him to say whether they were or were not acquainted with the system of private ownership. Do not forget, moreover, that chapter xxvi. follows chapter xxv., where Tacitus has said that the soil is cultivated by slaves, each paying certain dues to his master. After a sort of parenthesis on the freedmen, he returns to these *cultures.* He shows how they farm, and he blames their method. The chapter ought to be closely examined and translated word for word with the meaning each word had in the time of Tacitus, and not hastily rendered to suit some preconceived idea.

meaning of the word *consors*), he shall pay fifteen *solidi*... The boundary of the two estates, *terminatio*, is formed by distinct landmarks, such as little mounds or stones... If a man overstep this boundary, *marca*, and enters the property of another,[1] he shall pay the fine mentioned above." Thus, what the law calls *terminatio* in one line and *marca* in the next is clearly one and the same thing: it is the boundary which separates two private properties. A fact like this upsets Maurer's whole system.

Let us turn to the codes of the Germans who remained in Germany proper. The word *mark* is not to be met with throughout the Thuringian, Frisian and Saxon codes. It does occur in those of the Alamanni and Bavarians; but, instead of signifying a common territory, as Maurer would have it, it is used for the boundary of a territory. The laws of the Alamanni lay down that anyone who seizes a free man and sells him across the borders, *extra*

---

[1] *In sortem alterius fuerit ingressus.* In the documents from the 4th to the 8th century the word *sors* meant a private property: *sors patrimonium significat*, says the grammarian Festus. The contribution of corn is proportional, says the Theodosian code, to the extent of the properties, *pro modo sortium*, xi. 1, 15. Cassiodorus, *Letters*, viii. 26: *sortes propriæ*. Laws of the Visigoths, viii. 8, 5: *sortem suam claudere*, x. 1, 7: *terra in qua sortem non habet.* Salic law, Behrend, p. 112: *Si quis in mansionem aut sortem.* Law of the Burgundians, xlvii. 3: *Filii sortem parentum vel facultatem vindicabunt; lxxviii.: Si pater cum filiis sortem suam diviserit.* In all these examples *sors* signifies property or inheritance.

terminum, shall restore him to his country and pay a fine of forty *solidi*; immediately after, in the following line, comes a similar direction in case of the sale of a free woman beyond the borders, and the only difference is, that in place of *extra terminos* we have the phrase *extra marcam*: the two expressions are, we see, synonymous, and both denote a frontier.[1]

The Bavarian law indicates still more clearly the meaning of the word. Speaking of a man who takes a slave over the borders, it expresses it by *extra terminos hoc est extra marcam*.[2] It is impossible more clearly to indicate that the German word *mark* is synonymous with the Latin word *terminus*. Another passage from the Bavarian laws proves that *mark* was also used for the boundary of a private estate. Under the rubric, *De terminis ruptis*, it says that if two neighbours are at variance about their boundary, the judges ought first to examine whether the boundary is indicated by visible landmarks, such as marks on trees, hillocks or rivers. Now these two neighbours who have a common boundary are termed in the law *commarcani*.[3] Maurer, it is true, supposes that by this word is meant "men who dwelt in the same mark, the same common territory," but he would not have fallen into this error had he noticed that the same clause in the very next line

[1] *Lex Alamannorum*, xlv. and xlvi. edit. Pertz, p. 61; edit. Lehmann, pp. 105-106.

[2] *Lex Baiuwariorum*, xiii, 9, Pertz, p. 316.

[3] *Ibidem*, xii, 8, Pertz, p. 312.

expressly tells us that we have here to do with private property, with land that has been inherited; for each of the disputants makes a declaration that he has inherited his lands from his ancestors.[1] Here we have, then, precisely the opposite of mark in the sense of land held in common. Two neighbouring land-owners are at law about their boundaries. *Commarcani* is analogous to *confines*, which we find elsewhere; it is used of two men who have the same *marca*, the same *finis*, that is, a common boundary.

That the *mark* was a district possessed in common by a number of persons there is not a trace in German law. But are there not, at any rate, vestiges of some kind of common ownership? Maurer maintains that there are; and as evidence brings forward three instances, all taken from the Burgundian law: in section 13 he finds the words *in silva communi;* in section 31, *in communi campo;* and in section 1 of the "additamentum," *silvarum et pascuorum communionem.*[2] This is quite sufficient to convince some readers. Is not the word *communis* enough? And yet, let us make sure of our quotations, and with each of them let us look at the context.

---

[1] *Ibidem:* " Hucusque antecessores mei tenuerunt et in alodem mihi reliquerunt." The word *alodis* in the language of this period has no other meaning but inheritance. [On the meaning of *alod* see chap. iv. in the author's work *L'Alleu et le Domaine Rural,* which has appeared since his death.]

[2] Maurer, *Einleitung,* pp. 87, 88 and 145.

Article 13 does not in the least refer to a forest common to all, but to one which happens to be held in common between a Roman and a Burgundian, probably in consequence of the division of an estate which had belonged to the former.[1] This is a very different thing from a system of community. The passage shows, on the contrary, that in this case the forest was the property of two men. The mention in section 31 of a *campus communis* has led Maurer to say " that there were still in Gaul many fields which remained undivided." This is a mistake; for here again it is a field belonging to two proprietors that is spoken of; one which is only undivided so far as these two men are concerned. Anyone who has planted a vine in a common field shall make up for it to the other owner by handing over to him an equal extent of ground;[2] but if the co-proprietor from the first objected to his doing it, and the other has planted his vine in spite of him, he shall lose his pains and the vine shall belong to the owner of the field.[3] It is plain that here we have to do with something very different from a piece of ground com-

<hr />

[1] "Si quis tam burgundio quam romanus in silva communi exartum fecerit, aliud tantum spatii de silva hospiti suo consignet, et exartum quod fecit, remota hospitis communione, possideat."

[2] " Quicumque in communi campo vineam plantaverit, similem campum illi restituat in cujus campo vineam posuit."

[3] " Si vero post interdictum in campo alterius vineam plantare praesumpserit, laborem suum perdat, et vineam cujus est campus accipiat.

mon to an entire village. Maurer has, in this instance, made the mistake of isolating two words instead of reading the whole passage. As to his third quotation, section 1 of the *additamentum*, we find that this does not belong to Burgundian law. It belongs to the *Roman law* of the Burgundians; which is a very different thing.[1] It is, in fact, connected with an arrangement entirely Roman in its character, which is to be met with also in the code of Theodosius, according to which forest and pasturage might be held in common by a certain number of owners of land in tillage. The Roman law enacts that in such a case each owner should have rights over the forest and pasturage in proportion to the extent of his cultivated land.[2]

Thus we find that the three passages from German law, which Maurer believes he has discovered to prove the existence of a system of common ownership, either belong to Roman law or have no connection with this supposed common ownership of land, and even give positive proof of private ownership. In the same way finding somewhere the word *consortes*, he exclaims:

[1] See the note in the edition of Pertz, p. 607; see also Binding, in the *Fontes rerum Bernensium*, I. p. 142.

[2] " Silvarum, montium, et pascui unicuique pro rata possessionis suppetit esse commune." The same rule is to be found in another form in the law of the Burgundians, tit. 67: " Quicumque agrum vel colonicas tenent, secundum terrarum modum vel possessionis suae ratam, sic silvam inter se noverint dividendam." Neither in the one passage nor in the other is there any reference to a forest common to all.

' Here we have the associates of the mark " (p. 145),
and he again quotes a passage from the Burgundian
law ; but, as in the instance given above, we find that
the passage belongs to Roman law, and, on looking
at it, we see that the word *consortes* is used in the
Roman sense of co-heirs.[1] The meaning of the
clause is that if two or more co-heirs have not yet
divided the estate and apportioned their shares,
and one of them demands a division of the property,
it is not to be refused him.[2] In this case, again,
we are far enough away from a system of community
in land.

Such are the four passages which Maurer
finds, or thinks he finds, in German law ; and he
can only use them in support of his theory by
misinterpreting them. The whole body of German law is, in fact, a law in which private
property reigns supreme. Look at the Burgundian
law, and you will find mention of corn fields which

---

[1] *Lex romana Burgund.*, ed. Pertz, p. 607, Binding p. 142 ;
"Agri communia, nullis terminis limitati, exequationem inter
consortes nullo tempore denegandam." As to the synonymous
use of *consortes* and of *cohaeredes*, see Cicero, in *Verrem*, III., 23 ;
Paul, in the *Digest*, xxvii, 1., 31 ; Sidonius, *Letters* iv., 24 ;
and many other examples.

[2] Compare the sections *De familia herciscunda* in the *Digest*,
x. 2, and in the *Code* of Justinian, iii. 36 ; see also in the *Code* of
Justinian, the section iii. 37, *de communi dividundo*, and especially
the law No. 5.

D

are enclosed, and even of meadows ; the forest itself is
an object of private property. "If a Burgundian or
a Roman possess no forest, he may take dead wood
from the forest of another, and he *to whom the forest
belongs*, shall not hinder him ; but if he takes a tree
bearing fruit, he shall pay a fine to the owner, *domino
silvæ*."[1] A right of use, limited besides to dead wood,
is not the same thing as common ownership. It will
be noticed also that the term used in the code
for a country domain is *villa*, with its boundaries,
termini villæ.[2] Even the lands given by the king to
his servants are marked off by definite boundaries.[3]
These boundaries are sacred ; the Burgundian law-
giver lays down that any one who removes a boundary
shall lose his hand. It never for a moment entered
into the minds of the Burgundians to establish
agrarian communism.

In the law of the Visigoths, we find men who own
vineyards, fields, meadows, and even pasturage and
forests.[4] Land is hereditary property ; and there is
an entire section upon the division of landed posses-

---

[1] *Lex Burgundionum*, xxvii and xxviii., 1-2.

[2] *Ibidem*, xxxviii. 4 ; cf. xlix. 3 ; " dominus extra fines suos."

[3] *Ibidem*, lv. ; " ex ejus agri finibus quem barbarus cum
mancipiis publica largitione percepit." *Publica largitione*, by
the gift of the king. This is the meaning of the word *publicus*
in the language of the time.

[4] *Lex Wisigothorum*,, viii. 3, 15 ; viii. 5, 1 ; viii. 4, 27 ; "silvæ
dominus ; is cujus pascua sunt."

sions amongst co-heirs, as well as one on the boundaries of private estates. It is the same throughout the Lombard law; the right of ownership applies to everything, even to forests.[1] The owner of the land—*dominus*—has the right of selling it.[2] He can also let it on lease, *libellario nomine.*

The Salic law is a much less complete code than those we have been considering. It makes no mention of sale; but it contains the rule of hereditary succession. Land passes from father to son.[3] We also find enclosed corn fields and meadows,—a state of things hardly to be reconciled with community of land;[4] there are even forests which are one man's property, and where no one has the right of getting wood.[5]

The Ripuarian law indicates the use of hedges and enclosures; it recognises the right of hereditary succession to land, and also the power of disposing of it by sale.[6] All these are unmistakable signs of the prevalence of private ownership.

The hastiest glance at the law of the Alamanni,

---

[1] *Les Langobardorum*, Rotharis, 240.

[2] *Ibidem*, Liutprand, 116 ; Rotharis, 173.

[3] *Lex salica*, 59 ; "Si quis mortuus fuerit et filios non dimiserit." These words, with which the chapter begins, manifestly imply that the inheritance goes first to the son; sect. 5 ; "De terra nulla in muliere hereditas ; ad virilem sexum tota terra pertineat."

[4] *Ibidem*, ix. 4 ; Wolfenbuttel MS., ix. 9 ; cf. xvi. 5 ; xxxiv. 1.

[5] *Ibidem*, xxvii. 18. [6] *Lex Ripuaria*, 43, 58, 60, &c.

makes it absolutely clear that the soil was an object
of private property throughout the district in which it
was in force. We see from the first section that an individual might be so completely owner of his land that
he could, by a mere act of will, give it away to a church;
he had not to ask the leave of any group of associates.
Ownership of land is spoken of as *proprietas* and it is
"perpetual."[1] It is also hereditary; for the same
law shows that if this man did not give his land to
the church, it would pass "to his heirs;"[2] and it
provides for the case of one of the heirs object-
ing to the gift, without mentioning the possibility
that an "association of the mark" might lay claim
to the land. The same code also mentions mills
and water courses as objects of private property.[3]
The following clause enlightens us still more as to the
condition of the land: If a dispute arises between
two families concerning the boundary of their lands,
the two families fight in presence of the count; the
one to whom God gives the victory enters into
possession of the disputed territory; the members of
the other family pay a fine of 12 solidi "because
they have attacked *the property* of another."[4] Here

[1] *Lex Alamannorum* 1 ; proprietas in perpetuo permaneat.
[2] *Ibidem*, 2 ; si ipso qui dedit vel aliquis de heredibus suis. . .
Cf. *ibid.*, 57.
[3] *Ibidem*, 80 (83), edit. Lehmann, pp. 144, 145.
[4] *Lex Alamannorum*, art. 81 (84), edit Lehmann, pp. 145,
146. Pertz 113 and 163.

we have a law which cannot apply to lands common to all. It is clearly dealing with property which is permanent, and sharply defined; though it is property which belongs not so much to the individual as to the family. Among the Alamanni, as we see, traces of family ownership still survived.

In Bavarian law property in land is hereditary Each domain is surrounded by a boundary made "either by a bank of earth, or by stones stuck in the ground, or by trees marked with some particular sign."[1] And we must not suppose that these boundaries merely enclosed gardens; they enclosed fields and vineyards. "He who, whilst tilling his field or planting his vine, has unwittingly moved a land mark, shall restore it in the presence of his neighbours." "When two neighbours having a common boundary have a dispute, if the land marks are not clear, the one says, 'My ancestors possessed the land as far as this line, and left it me by inheritance:' and the other protests and maintains that the land belonged to his ancestors as far as some other line; then the dispute is settled by judicial combat."[2] This is a good instance of individual ownership. Ownership has long been hereditary; since each of the litigants says he has received his estate from his ancestors, and the lands have been held by the same families for several generations. Nor

[1] *Lex Baiuvariorum*, xii. 4.
[2] *Ibidem*, xii. 4, Pertz, p. 311.

is it only to land under tillage that the right of ownership applies; it applies equally to forests and pastures; to uncultivated as well as to cultivated land: "If any one sells his property, whether cultivated land, or uncultivated, meadows or forests, the sale ought to be transacted in writing and before witnesses."[1]

In Thuringian law, land passes from father to son. Saxon law also recognises the right of private property; and authorises the sale and gift of land.

The capitularies of the Merovingian kings, again, show that private property was the normal and regular state of things. An edict of Chilperic declares that land shall pass not only to the son according to the ancient rule, but also to the daughter, brother, or sister. In his treatment of this last point Maurer once more displays singular inaccuracy. From this law which declares the rule of hereditary succession, he draws the conclusion that before that time there had been community of property. The edict of Chilperic says that in no case shall the neighbours take possession of the land; this appears to him to mean that, up to the day this law was made, the neighbours were the real owners, and inherited before the son of the dead man. He does not notice that it is precisely in the case where a son survives that Chilperic contents himself with referring to the ancient rule of hereditary succes-ion. The

[1] *Ibidem*, xvi., 2. Pertz, p. 321 ; cf. *ibid.* 15, and xxii. p. 332.

words *non vicini* occur in the paragraph which deals with the case of the death of the owner without children. To say that if a man dies without children, the nearest heirs must be sought for, and the neighbours are not to take possession of the land, is not the same as saying that until that time the neighbours had had rights over the land. To exaggerate the meaning of a quotation to such a point as this is really to pervert it.[1] Not a single Frankish capitulary, not a single law, charter, or formula, mentions this imaginary "right of the neighbours" over the land. Not one of these documents even alludes to a village holding its land in common. The Carolinginian capitularies, which were drawn up for Germany as well as for Gaul, recognise two methods only of land-holding, the allodial, *i.e.*, complete and heritable ownership; and beneficiary, *i.e.*, land granted by its owner for a time and under certain conditions. They know nothing of community of ownership.

If one could point anywhere to an annual or periodical division of the soil this would be a proof of agrarian communism. Maurer accordingly maintains (page 8) that this annual division was, as a matter of fact, for a long time practised. In support of

---

[1] M. Viollet copies Maurer, but forces the meaning still further : " King Chilperic," says he, " was obliged to declare that the neighbours should not succeed and that the sons should " (*Bibl. de l'École des Chartes*, 1872, p. 492). Such an interpretation is the very opposite of the original.

so grave an assertion, to prove an historical fact
of such magnitude, we might hope that he would
furnish us with numerous and precise references.
He gives but one, a document of the year 815,
printed in Neugart's *Codex diplomaticus*, No. 182.[1]
Now look at this deed; it is a gift made to a convent
by a certain Wolfin. Read it through; you will not
find a single mention of community, a single mention
of a yearly division. Wolfin is a land-owner; the
lands he grants are his property; even more than
that, they are his by inheritance; they have descended to him from his father. Here then we have
a deed which from its first word to the last proves the
existence of private property, and shows the very
opposite of common ownership.

How has Maurer managed to find in this a con-
firmation of his theory? We have here a striking
example of the light-hearted way in which he works.
The donor, in making a list according to custom of the
lands he is giving, writes *terræ anales, prata, vineæ,
pascua.* Maurer lays hold of this word *anales.* Of
course, it is not Latin; so he begins by supposing
that the copyist made a mistake, and corrects it to
annales. But even the word *annalis* does not belong to the language of legal documents; there is not a
single other instance of its use. Maurer supposes that it
means "lands that are held for only one year." But

---

[1] Neugart, i. p. 153.

that is impossible; since, according to this very deed,
they are Wolfin's property by inheritance. The whole
list, *terra anales, prata, vineœ, pascua* relates beyond
doubt to inherited property. The word *anales* is
puzzling; but any one who is familiar with charters
of this kind must have often observed in those of this
period the expression *terra areales* taking the place of
terra arabiles,[1] but with the same meaning, *i.e.*, arable
lands. It occurs frequently in deeds of gift. When in
a number of documents exactly alike in phraseology
you find in eighty *terra arabiles, prata, vineœ,
silva, pascua,* and in twenty more *terra ariales,
prata, vineœ, silva, pascua*; then, supposing in a
single example you meet with *terra anales, prata,
vineœ, silva, pascua,* common sense tells you that this
word *anales,* which, however we take it, is incorrect,
was written for *ariales,* and that either the editor or
the copyist made a mistake. There is no doubt
whatever that the donor makes a gift of "lands he
possesses by inheritance," which include "arable lands,
meadows, vineyards and pasture." Such is the deed
of 815; and it is an illustration of the method Maurer
follows. He cites a deed, which, taken as a whole, proves
the existence of private and heritable property; he

---

[1] The words *terra areales* or *ariales* are to be found especially
in the *Codex Fuldensis* of Dronke, Nos. 16, 78, 155, etc., and in
the *Traditiones possessionesque Wizenburgenses* of Zeuss, Nos. 9,
35, 52, etc.

does not tell the reader this, but picks out from its context a single word; alters it and translates it in his own way; and presenting the reader only with this one word, tries to make him believe that the deed proves the annual division and common ownership of land.

When Maurer comes to deal with the barbarian invasions, he takes great pains to get together a number of quotations which will suggest the idea of a partition of land (pages 72 *seq.*); but if we examine them, we see that there is absolutely nothing about a *yearly* or *periodical* division. He first quotes from Victor Vitensis, who tells us that Genseric, directly he was master of the province called Zeugitana, divided its soil amongst his soldiers " in hereditary lots."[1]   This is exactly the opposite of a yearly division of land, and, consequently, of common ownership.   Next comes Procopius who writes that " the Ostrogoths divided amongst themselves the lands which had before been given to the Heruli."[2] Here again we have to do with a division of land among private owners.   Then Maurer, with a great profusion of quotations, points to the divisions of property that many scholars believe were effected between the Roman proprietors on the one hand and

---

[1] Victor Vitensis, i. 4 ; " Exercitui provinciam Zeugitanam funicuo hereditates divisit.'

[2] Procopius, *Gothic War,* i. 1.

the Visigoths, Burgundians and Franks on the other.
But this division, in any case, was neither yearly nor
periodical. Each portion became, from the very first
day, permanent and hereditary. It would be childish
to maintain that a division of this kind was the sign
of a system of common ownership. It shows on the
contrary that the new comers knew nothing about
community in land, and never practised it.

And so we find that Maurer cannot, from all these
nations, produce a single instance of a village holding
its land in common or of an association of the mark.
Not a single instance either from writers of the time,
or from codes of law, or from charters, or from legal
formulæ. And it is impossible to reply that this is
simply a case of omission ; for in these laws, charters
and formulae, we not only do not find common ownership, but we do find exactly the opposite ; we find
signs everywhere of private property, and of the
rights of inheritance, donation and sale.

There is not even a trace to be found in these codes
of law of an earlier system of non-division. When
they lay down that land is hereditary, or that it
can be sold, they do not say that this was a novelty.
It is easy for Maurer to declare that these practices
were borrowed from Roman law; this is a convenient
hypothesis, but one for which there is no proof. The
fact is that the earlier condition of things, of which
we can see the traces in German legislation, was not com-

munism, but the common ownership of the *family*. We find signs of this in the Salic and in the Ripuarian law, and in the codes of the Burgundians and Thuringians. The revolution in the land system which took place at this period was a change not from common ownership to private ownership, but from the ownership of the family to that of the individual. The practices of bequest and of sale are the chief marks of this great change; and it is this alone that we can attribute to the influence of Roman law: while even here it seems to me that it would be safer to regard it rather as a natural process of evolution which has taken place in every nation.

If in German law Maurer can discover no trace of the mark or of community in land, what are the documents on which he rests his proof of their existence? If we study his book with some attention, we shall be surprised to find that he goes for his authorities to the *Traditiones*, under which title are classed the various collections of charters of the 8th to the 14th centuries.[1] But all

[1] The chief of these collections are the *Codex Diplomaticus* and the *Syllogi* of Guden, 1728, 1743 ; the *Codex traditionum Corbeiensium* of Falke, 1752 ; the *Monumenta Boica*, beginning in 1763 ; the *Codex Laureshamensis abbatiæ diplomaticus*, 1768 ; the *Subsidia* and the *Nova Subsidia diplomatica* of Wurdtwein, 1772-1781 ; the *Codex diplomaticus Alemanniæ* of Neugart, 1791 ; the *Urkundenbuch* for the history of the Lower Rhine district by Lacomblet, 1840 ; the *Traditiones Wissemburgenses* of Zeuss, 1842 ; the *Traditiones Fuldenses* of Dronke, 1844 ; and by

these, and they number almost ten thousand, are,
without exception, deeds of private property. In
fact, they are always either deeds of gift, or of sale,
or of exchange, or of the grant of *precaria*. It is impossible not to allow that the thousands of deeds of this
kind are so many proofs of private property, since
you can neither sell nor give away what is not already
your own. Amongst these collections we also find
judicial decisions, and they all point in the same
direction.

Observe, too, that there is absolutely no doubt as to
the meaning of the language employed. Could
language be clearer than that of the following passage
taken from a deed of 770 ? " I, Wiebert, give to the
church of St. Nazarius the farms (*mansi*), lands,
fields, meadows and slaves that belong to me. All
these I deliver to the church to be held for ever, with
the right and power of holding, giving, exchanging,
and doing with them as seems to it best.' [1] Or of a

the same editor, the *Codex diplomaticus Fuldensis*, 1850. Add to
these certain works wherein a great number of similar documents
have been printed : Meicholbeck, *Historia Frisingensis*, 1724 ;
Hontheim, *Historia Trevirensis diplomatica*, 1750 ; Schœpflin,
Alsatia diplomatica, 1772 ; Wigand, *Archiv für Geschichte West-
phalens*, 1826 ; Bodmann, *Rheingauische Alterthümer*, 1819 ;
Mone, *Zeitschrift für die Geschichte des Oberrheins*, 1850. Since
Maurer wrote, several other collections have been printed,
especially those of Beyer, *Urkundenbuch . . . ., mittelrheinischen
Territorien*, 1860 ; Bünding, *Fontes rerum Hennensium*, 1863 ; and
the *Urkundenbuch der Abtei S. Gallen*, 1863.

[1] *Codex Laureshamensis* No. 11, p. 25-26 : " Ego Wigbertus

deed of 786 : " I, daughter of Theodon, give to St.
Nazarius all that I hold by inheritance in the places
here mentioned; and everything that has been in my
possession and ownership, I hand over into the possession and ownership of St. Nazarius."[1]   And again :
" Whatever land belongs to me I give to the abbot
and his successors to hold and possess it for ever ; "[2]
and yet again : " I, Wrachaire, give whatever land is
mine in my own right for the abbot henceforward to
hold in his own right, *jure proprio.*"[3]   These expressions occur in thousands of documents.   Often the
donor or seller adds that he holds the land by inheritance, that he has received it from his father.[4]   An-
dono ad Sanctum Nazarium, .. in mansis, terris, campis, pratis,
.. quantumcunque in his locis proprium habere videor .. dono
trado atque transfundo perpetualiter ad possidendum, jure et
potestate habendi, tenendi, donandi, commutandi, vel quidquid
exinde facere volueritis liberam ac firmissimam habeatis potestatem."

[1] *Codex Laureshamensis,* No. 12: "Dono ad Sanctum Nazarium
. . . de propria alode nostra in locis nuncupatis. . . ubicunque
moderno tempore mea videtur esse possessio vel dominatio, de
jure meo in jus ac dominationem S. Nazarii dono trado atque
transfundo."

[2] Neugart, p. 401, anno 879 : " Donamus. . . ut perpetualiter
teneant atque possideant."   Meichelbeck, pp. 48 and 53 of the
Instrumenta ; " Donamus. . . rem propriam nostram ;" p. 67 :
"propriam alodem ;" p. 36 : "rem propriam. . . in possessionem
perpetuam."

[3] Lacomblet, No. 4.

[4] Meichelbeck, *Instrumenta,* p. 27 : " Ego Chunipertus propriam hereditatem quam genitor meus mihi in hereditatem
reliquit."   Lacomblet, No. 8, anno 796 : "Omne quod mihi jure

other thing we must not fail to notice is that ownership is not limited to land under cultivation, it includes
forest, pasture and streams,[1] as we find over and
over again. And it is never a village community or
mark which makes such a gift, but always a single
individual.

Such is the character of the records Maurer sets about
using in order to prove the existence of community
in land in the Middle Ages. It is evident that,
taken as a whole, they are in direct contradiction
to this theory ; but what he does is to separate from
the rest about twenty deeds, take his evidence from
them, and ignore the existence of the rest. What
can be said for a proceeding by which, merely for the
sake of propping up a theory, certain isolated cases
are picked out, and the great mass of evidence,
which is in opposition to the theory, is passed over ?
At the very least, it would have been only fair to
warn the reader that the deeds quoted belonged to an

hereditario legibus obvenit in villa Bidnenghoim." Neugart,
No. 306, anno 843 ; " Quidquid proprietatis in Alemannia
visus sum habere, sive ex paterna hereditate seu ex acquisito,
sive divisum habeam cum meis coheredibus seu indivisum. . . id
est domibus, edificiis, mancipiis, campis, pomiferis, pratis, pascuis, silvis, viis, aquis, cultis et incultis."

[1] Meichelbeck, p. 27, document of the 8th century: " Tradidi
territorium, prata, pascua, aquarum decursibus, silvis, virgultis,
omne cultum aut non cultum, in possessionem perpetuam."
Lacomblet, No. 4, anno 794 : " Terram proprii juris mei. . . cum
silvis, pratis, pascuis, perviis, aquis."

insignificant minority—eighteen or twenty out of
about ten thousand. Readers have not always
volumes of this kind at their elbow; and if they have,
it does not occur to them to verify the references. If
you present them with twenty quotations, they at once
suppose that these are the only ones in existence.
They ought to be told that there are ten thousand
other deeds of the same character, written at the same
time, drawn up according to the same forms. You
should confess that these ten thousand deeds say
exactly the opposite of the twenty you quote. You
should not leave them in ignorance of the fact that
these thousands of gifts, wills, sales or exchanges of
land form an absolute proof of a system of private property. Only after pointing all this out, would it be
right to tell them that there are perhaps eighteen or
twenty deeds in which some signs of community in land
may possibly be seen. No avowal of this kind was,
however, made by Maurer; his followers in Germany
and France have been equally silent. All of them
calmly appeal to the *Traditiones*, as if these fifteen
ponderous volumes were not in themselves an over-
whelming refutation of their theory.

We must go further. Are the eighteen or twenty
deeds referred to by Maurer given correctly? Do
they really mean what our author wishes them to
mean? Observe that he never quotes more than a
single line, sometimes only one or two words. We

must go to the documents themselves and verify them.[1]

He first of all quotes, on page 47, a deed from the Laurch collection. It is a charter of 773, by which Charles the Great grants to that monastery in perpetuity, the villa of Hephenheim, including lands, houses, slaves, vineyards, forests, fields, meadows, pasture, water and streams, with all its appurtenances and dependances, its boundaries and its marks, *cum terminis et marchis suis.*[2] Here is the mark, says Maurer. Yes, but not the mark of the village community. It is precisely the opposite, the march or boundary of a private property. We have here to do with a villa, a domain which has been the private property of the king and is now becoming the property of a convent. There is not a thought here of common ownership, or of a common mark, or of a village association. There is not even a village. It is a domain, cultivated, says the charter, by slaves. *Cum terminis et marchis suis* are both words meaning the boundaries of the domain; and in a repetition of this kind there is nothing surprising. The *marca* is precisely the same as the *terminus.* We saw above, in the Bavarian law, *terminus id est marca.* In the same way a charter of Childeric II. describes the

---

[1] Not unduly to prolong this discussion we will leave on one side the documents of the 14th and 15th century. It will be enough to examine those of an earlier date.

[2] *Codex Laureshamensis,* No. 6, vol. i. p. 15.

boundary-line of a domain as *fines et marchas*.[1] We must not suppose that these *marchae* were a stretch of land separate from the domain. The expression *dono villam* . . . . *cum marchis* will astonish no one who is familiar with documents of this class. Any one who has any acquaintance with them knows that it was the custom in deeds of gift, or sale of a domain, to add, "with its boundaries." Charters written in Gaul have the phrase, *cum omni termino suo;* in Germany, *cum omni marca sua* or *cum marcis suis*.[2] In a large number of our documents *marca* is used in this sense alone, as, for instance, in the *Codex Fuldensis*, No. 21, a deed of 760, in which a certain person makes a gift of a villa *cum marcas et fines.*

Maurer refers to many other documents;[3] a charter of Louis the Pious, a deed of 748 given by Grandidier, six deeds of 768, 778, 790, 794, 796 and 811 quoted by Schœpflin, and a diploma of 812 in the collection of Neugart. But what do we gather from all this evidence ? Every one of these documents is a deed of donation in perpetuity; in every case it is the donation of land situated in a locality described indifferently as *villa, finis* or *marca: in fine vel in villa Berkheimmarca ; in fine vel marca Angehises-*

---

[1] *Diplomata*, edit. Pardessus, No. 341.

[2] See especially the charters of the Abbey of St. Gall, Nos 185, 186, 187, etc.

[3] Maurer, *Einleitung*, pp. 41, 42, 45.

heim; in villa vel in fine Haidersheim marca; in villa Oskarvillare are in ipsa marca; domo portionem earum quae ad in marca Odradasheim; in late et in marca Northeim; in marto vel in marca Ongisheim; quidquid in ipso loco et ipsa marca habet. All these expressions are synonymous and recur again and again. In 803 Amalfrid makes a gift of whatever he owns in marca vel villa Sethja and also in villa vel marca Baldavia[1] All these quotations prove no more than this, that the word mark, after being originally used in the sense of a boundary of a domain, afterwards came to mean the domain itself; a change in the use of a word, which is familiar enough to students of philology. The same thing has happened with the synonymous terms finis and terminus. In Gaul, villa Klarinous and terminus Klarinous are used indifferently; as are Longoviana villa and Longoviana finis. In Germany villa or marca are used in the same way. In the examples given by Maurer, I recognise the existence of the mark, but of a mark which was the same thing as a villa, that is a private estate.[2] Maurer has mistaken private domains for common lands.

[1] Codex Laureshamensis, No. 24, i. pp. 70, 71.
[2] Sometimes a great marca contains several hamlets (dörfer); as in Gaul the villa sometimes contains several vici. This will not surprise anyone who has examined the nature and extent of rural estates in the 8th century. In a document in the Codex Laureshamensis, vol. iii. p. 25, a marca includes several villae. This case is rare, and does not change the nature of the mark.

In the thousands of documents in the collections of the *Traditiones* the name of the domain, which the donor owns either in whole or part, is always given. And we may say that, roughly speaking, out of eight instances we shall find it called *villa* seven times and *marca* once, and that there is no other difference between the two sets of documents.

Another fact has escaped Maurer's notice, and that is that these marks frequently bear the name of their owner. It is well known that this was the usual custom with the *villæ* of Gaul,—*villa Floriacus, villa Latiniacus, Maurovilla, Maurovillare;* and in the same way we have many instances of names like *marca Angehises, marca Baldanis, marca Munefridi, marca Warcharenheim, Droctegisomarca.* The resemblance is noteworthy. In the study of history observation is worth more than all the theories in the world.

Occasionally the word *mark* denotes something larger than an estate, and is applied to an entire province. What is the origin of this? In the documents of the sixth and seventh centuries, in the writings of Marius of Avenches, in the laws of the Alamanni and in those of the Bavarians, and later on in the capitularies of Charles the Great, *marca* signified the frontier of a country.[1] Little by little this word began

----

[1] *Marii Arentici chronicon,* ed. Arndt, p. 15. *Lex Alamannorum,* xlvii. *Lex Baiuvariorum,* xiii., 9, Pertz, p. 316.

to mean border-country, and so arose the expression "the marches" of Spain, of Brittany, Carinthia, Austria, Brandenburg; until almost every country had insensibly grown into a "march." Must we suppose from this, as Maurer would maintain, that the whole German territory was mark-land from the very first? Not at all. We know the origin of each of these marches, and almost the exact date at which they came into existence. One belongs to the ninth century, another to the tenth, and another was not created until the eleventh. To refer them to a remote period of antiquity is an error which might easily have been avoided.[1]

We may allow that Maurer proves easily and with abundant evidence that the word *marca* was often used; but what he had to prove was that this *marca* meant land held in common, and for this he has not, up to this point, given the slightest evidence.

There are, on the contrary, thousands of documents showing that lands within the mark were held as private property, and not in common. In a deed of 711, Ermanrad gives away in perpetuity "thirty acres

Capitulary of 799, art. 19; of 803; of 811; edit. Borétius, pp. 51, 139, 167.

[1] Maurer seems to me to have made another mistake in identifying *mark* with *gau* (p. 59). No document gives the two terms as synonymous; on the contrary, there are hundreds of documents which tell us that such and such a *mark* is situated in such and such a *pagus*, which shows clearly enough that *marca* and *pagus* are not the same thing.

which he owns in the *marca Munefred*," and he adds
that this land is his "by inheritance from his grand-
mother."[1]   Another makes a gift "of all he owns in
the *marca Bellunis*, whether inherited from his father
or his mother."[2]   Maurer is ready to admit that arable
land was held as private property, but he will not allow
that meadows and forests could be held in the same
way.   We have seen, however, in documents of the
eighth or ninth centuries, that forests and pastures were
given away or sold in perpetuity, as well as arable
land.[3]   In 793 Ruchilde makes a gift " of all that is
his property in the *marca* Dinenheimer; and this includes *mansi*, fields, meadows, pastures, waters, and
streams."[4]   Meginhaire, to take another case, gives
what he possesses in the villa Frankenheim and
mentions " fields, *mansi*, meadows, pastures, forests
and streams."[5]   The same thing is repeated in thousands
of documents;[6] showing that a system of private

[1] *Diplomata*, ed. Pardessus, ii. p. 434.

[2] *Ibidem*, ii. 440.

[3] Schœpflin, *Alsat. diplom.*, i. p. 13, a charter of the year 730,
wherein Theodo sells all that he possesses in the *marca* Hameris-
tad, "quantum in ipso fine est, ea ratione ut ab hac die habeatis
ipsas terras et silvas. . . . et quidquid exindo facere volueritis
liberam habeatis potestatem."

[4] *Codex Laureshamensis*, No. 15, v. i. p. 34.

[5] *Tradit. Wissemburgenses*, No. 127.

[6] See for example a charter of the 8th century, where we
read : "Ego Oda dono in Pingumarca quidquid proprietatis
habeo, id est, terris, vineis, pratis, silvis, totum et integrum."
(*Codex Fuldensis*, No. xv. p. 11.)—Neugart, i. p. 301, an exchange

ownership was in force in the mark, as well as in the villa, and that it extended to lands of every description.

This is the conclusion to which we are brought by the twenty documents from the collections of *Tradi-tiones* referred to by Maurer. Not one of them shows a trace of a community of the mark or of any other community. All the twenty, like the thousands of documents Maurer passes over, are simply deeds relating to private property.

It is, then, indisputable that all existing documents show us a system of private property; but Maurer supposes, 1st, that there must once have been a period of undivided common property; 2nd, that the "associates of the mark" passed from this to the later system of private ownership, by dividing the land amongst them. That property had ever been undivided he has no kind of proof to bring forward. It is a statement he frequently repeats as if he had already proved it, but we shall search his book in vain for any such demonstration. It is certainly very strange for a scholar to heap together evidence for a host of matters of secondary importance, and neglect to bring forward a single authority for that on which everything turns, i.e., the existence of the

of 858: "Dedit 106 juchos de terra arabili et de silva 140 juchos, et accepit a Willelmo in eadem marcha qunaquid ex paterno jure habebat, id est 106 juchos de terra arabili cum omnibus appenditiis, silvis, viis, alpibus, aquis."

primitive community. His book is rich in references, but not one bears upon this; so that we might
say that everything here is proved except the very
point that was in need of proof.

As evidence of the supposed partition by means
of which the "associates of the mark" passed
to a system of private ownership, Maurer refers
to three authorities.[1] The first is the hagiographer
Meginarius, who, in his *Translatio Alexandri*,
relates a tradition according to which the Saxons, on
getting possession of Thuringia, at once divided the
country amongst themselves into separate portions to
be held in perpetuity, and handed over parts of them
to be cultivated by *coloni*.[2] Here we certainly have
an instance of a division of land; but this division does not follow upon a condition of undivided ownership; so far from implying the existence of such a state of things, it shows rather that
to these Saxons the very idea is unknown. As soon

[1] Maurer, *Einleitung*, pages 73, and 80.
[2] Read the whole passage. *Translatio S. Alexandri*, in
Pertz, vol. ii. p. 675, "Eo tempore quo Theodoricus rex Francorum,
contra Irmenfredum, ducem Thuringorum, dimicans . . . conduxit Saxones in adjutorium, promissis pro victoria habitandi
sedibus. . . Terram juxta pollicitationem suam iis delegavit.
Qui eam sorte dividentes, partem illius colonis tradiderunt,
singuli pro sorte sua sub tributo exercendam; cetera vero loca
ipsi possederunt." Do not forget that the word *sors* is the usual
term in the language of the period for property. The narrative
shows clearly that it is a division made for ever that is
here described.

as they are masters of the soil they establish a system
of private property. The same fact is illustrated by the
passage from Helmold, which Maurer quotes, where we
are told that certain Westphalians, on being settled in a
conquered country, at once divided it between them.[1]
His third reference is to a Bavarian document of the
year 1247, where we are told that "the fields were divided
by a line, and twelve acres allotted to each house." Maurer imagines this refers to an association of free peasants
who have for centuries cultivated the soil in common,
and at last divide it amongst themselves in equal shares.
Not at all. If we read the whole document we see
that it refers to a villa, that is to say, a large estate
belonging to a single proprietor, who distributes the
soil in holdings amongst his *rustici*.[2] The document
is interesting as illustrating a very common usage,
according to which every peasant received three lots

[1] Helmold, *chr. Slav.* i. c. 91 : "Adduxit multitudinem populorum de Westphalia, ut incolerent terram Polaborum, et divisit
eis terram in funiculo distributionis."

[2] Charter of 1247 in the *Monumenta Boica*, vol. xi. p. 53.
The estate in question is the *villa* Yserhofen. Its owner is the
Abbot of Niederalteich : "Cum ad hoc devenisset quod agros et
prata, quia diu sine colonis exstiterant, nullus sciret. . . rustici
exclamis pro quantitate et limitibus contenderent. Ego Her-
mannus abbas. . . compromissum fuit ut maximus campus per
funiculos mensuraretur et cuilibet huber 12 jugera deputarentur
. . . in totidem partes aequalibus campus et tertim divideretur. . .
Inchoata est ista divisio per Alwinum monachum ac bonorum et
fratrem Bertholdum prepositum et Rudolfum officialem cum
funiculis mensurantem."

of land, one in each of the three different kinds.[1]   This
is, however, a very different thing from the division
among common owners of land hitherto undivided;
it is a division amongst tenants, carried out by the
proprietor.   Thus we see that not one of the documents referred to by Maurer points to a partition
amongst "associates of the mark," or to a partition which
replaced an earlier system of undivided property by one
of private ownership.   We must, accordingly, recognise
that it is a mere hypothesis to suppose that land was
ever held in common by a group of associates; that
the only established certain fact is the existence of
private property, which rests on the evidence of all
the laws and all the charters; and that there is
nothing to suggest that this state of things was the
outcome of a primitive system of community.   As far
back as the day when the word *mark* first appears in
documentary evidence, and throughout that evidence,
the system of private property is everywhere in possession of the field.

We would not say, however, that there are no examples of land held in common; and we must now
see what was the character of this common ownership.   It was of two sorts.   Of the first kind an
example is afforded by a document of 815 cited by
Maurer, in which occur the words *silvæ communi-*

---

[1] [M. Fustel uses the term "les trois catégories;" but
the *maximus campus*, *secundus*, and *tertius*, would point rather
to the "three-field system."]

uorm ; a certain Wighald makes a gift of a mansus, and of his share of a forest.[1]   Another example which he refers to is a forest belonging to three villæ in common.[2]   We are told also of a Count Hugo who bestows all his possessions in the villa of Brunno as well as "the three quarters of the *marca silvatica* which make up his share."[3]   Another less rich can only give a *huba*, but he gives at the same time the portion of the forest to which his huba has a right.[4] We might also refer to a case in which a forest was held in common by two proprietors of two domains down to the year 1184, when a division was effected by a judicial decision.[5]   There were, then, forests common to several persons ; but that does not justify us in saying that all forests were common to every one ; for we have documents without number in which a man gives away or sells a forest that clearly belongs to himself alone.   We must also remember that when

[1] *Codex Laureshamensis*, No. 106, p. 164.

[2] Wigand, *Archiv*, i. 2, p. 86.

[3] *Codex Lauresh.*, No. 69, p. 74 : "Quidquid de rebus propriis habere videbatur in villa Brunnen et tres partes de illa marca salvatica, portione videlicet sua."   I will explain elsewhere the meaning of *portio*.   All I need say at present is that this word, which occurs more than three hundred times in our authorities, always means a part belonging to an owner.   A *portio* is spoken of as *sold*, *bequeathed*, and *given*.

[4] Laurenblet, No. 7 : "Horum integram et scara in silva juxta furnam: horre pleno. . . jure hereditario."

[5] To be found in Mone, *Zeitschrift für Geschichte des Oberrheins*, vol. i. pp. 405-406.

we read that a forest was common, it does not mean
common to everyone, but only common to a *villa*, or
perhaps to two or three *villae*,[1] so that the owners of
these *villae* alone have any rights over it.[2] Now,
supposing several persons are joint-owners of a forest,
this is a very different thing from a system of community in land. Each of them has rights over the
forest exactly in proportion to the amount of his property.[3] "So much for every *huba*," says one document.
In another a man makes a gift of all he has inherited
in a villa, together with his share, a twelfth, of a forest.[4]
All the forests here spoken of are nothing more than
appendages to property. We must not be misled by
the expression "common forest;" which means no
more than that the forest was the property of several

[1] [As late as the 13th century in England "the typical struggle
as to common rights was not a struggle between lords and com-
moners, but a struggle between the men or the lords of two
different townships." Maitland, *Bracton's Note-Book*, I., 136.]

[2] This is to be found even in Roman law. See Scaevola, in
the *Digest*, viii. 5, 20 : "Plures ex municipibus, qui diversa
praedia possidebant, saltum communem, ut jus compascendi
haberent, mercati sunt, idque etiam a successoribus eorum ob-
servatum est."

[3] Deed of exchange of the year 871 in Neugart, No. 461, vol.
i. p. 377 : "Dedimus illi in proprietatem jugera 105 et de communi silva quantum ad portionem nostram pertinet. . . Et de
silva juxta estimationem nostrae portionis in communi silva."

[4] Lacomblet, No. 22, document of 801 : "Tradidi particulam
hereditatis meae in villa Englandi . . . et duodecimam partem in
silva Braclog."

persons exercising over it all the rights of ownership, even the right of selling their shares (as we see in hundreds of documents) without having to ask the leave of anyone, and without even consulting their fellow proprietors.

To the other class of instances belongs that referred to by Maurer (p. 93) from a document of the end of the eighth century, where again the words *silva communis* are to be found. The document relates to a large estate; and it shows that the estate included a forest, part of which was reserved for the lord, and the rest was common to the tenants.[1] We are here far removed from the community " of the associates of the mark," for in this instance the cultivators of the soil are merely tenants under a proprietor. Maurer quotes another deed of 1173, where we read : " In this forest none of us had anything of his own, but it was common to all the inhabitants of our villa "[2] This is another example, not of community of property, for it is tenants who are speaking, but of community in tenure. Following upon this are a series of quotations proving common use. " I give a *curtile* with rights of use in the forest, *cum usu silvatico*, that is with

---

[1] Kindlinger, *Münsterische Beiträge*, ii. 3 : " Est ibi silva communis. . . Silva domini quæ singularis est."

[2] Maurer, *Einleitung*, p. 115, following Bodmann, *Rheingauische Alterthümer*, i. 453 : " In hac silva nullus nostrum privatum habebat quidquid, sed communiter pertinebat ad omnes villæ nostræ insulas."

the privilege of gathering dead and broken wood." [1]
" We give such and such *curtilia* with all the rights
of use belonging to these *curtilia*." [2]   Rights of use,
in this instance, included the power of cutting wood
for fire or for the purpose of building, and also of
sending in pigs to feed on the acorns ; but a right of
use does not imply common ownership.[3]   Maurer's
supposition that the rights of use in certain forests
are survivals from a time when the forest belonged
to all, is a mere theory.   Reasoning *à priori*

[1] Deed of exchange of the year 905, Neugart, No. 653, vol. i.
p. 539 ; " Curtile unum . . . cum tali usu silvatico ut qui illic
sedent, sterilia et jacentia ligna licenter colligant." Cf. *Lex
Burgundionum*, xxviii. 1.

[2] Neugart, No. 624, vol. i. p. 511, acto de 896 : " Curtilia
quæ sunt sex et inter arvam terram et prata juchos 378, cum
omnibus usibus ad ipsa curtilia in eadem marcha (Johannis-
villare) pertinentibus."

[3] Alamannic formula, Rozière, No. 401 : " In silva lignorum
materiarumque cæsuram pastumque vel saginam animalium."
Lacomblet, No. 20 : "Cum pastu plenissimo juxta modulum
curtilis ipsius."   Neugart, No. 462 : "Tradidi quinque hobas et
quidquid ad illas pertinet et ad unamquamque hobam decem
porcos saginandos in proprietate mea in silva Lotstetin quando
ibi glandes inveniri possunt."   Mone, *Zeitschrift*, i. 395 : "Eodem
jure quo licitum est villanis. . . possunt oves suas vel alia ani-
malia pascere in communibus pascuis dictæ villae."   Schœpflin,
Alsatia dipl., ii. 49 : "Jus utendi lignis in silva Heingereite."
Codex Laureshamensis, No. 105, i. p. 164, anno 815 : "Tradidit
Alfger terram ad modia 10 sementis, et prata, et in illam silvam
porcos duos, et in Rosmalla mansum plenum cum pratis et in
silvam porcos sex."   Guden, *Codex dipl.*, i. 920 : " Universitas
rusticorum habet jus (in ea villa) secandi ligna pro suis usibus et
edificiis."

he does not think it possible that such rights
could have arisen in any other way. It is, however,
possible that they spring from a very different source,
and that a careful examination of a number of documents will show us what that was.

Let us take, for instance, a deed of 863, wherein
Count Anafrid gives his villa of Geizefurt to the
monastery of Lorsch. He gives a detailed account of
this property; which includes a lord's *mansus*, nineteen servile tenements and a forest, whose size is
measured by the fact that it can feed a thousand pigs.
The donor thinks he ought to put a clause in the deed
to the effect that his peasants have the use of the
forest; a use definitely regulated,—giving, for instance,
to some the right to send ten pigs, to others five, and
not including for any of them the right of cutting
wood.[1] It is clear that the forest, as well as the rest
of the domain, belongs to a proprietor; the domain is
cultivated by serfs, and the serfs have a certain

[1] *Codex Laureshamensis*, No. 34, vol. i. p. 68: "Ego Anefridus
. . . trado res proprietatis meæ in Odeheimero marca, in villa
Geizefurt, hoc est, mansum indominicatum habentem hobas 3,
et hubas serviles 19, et silvam in quam mittere possumus mille
porcos enginari, et quisquid in eadem marca villave habeo proprietatis, exceptis tribus hobis quam habet Wolfbrat et in eam-
dem silvam debet mittere porcos 10, alteram habet Thutulf,
tertiam Sigoburo et dobent mittere in silvam uterque porcos 10,
et nullam aliam utilitatem sive ad extirpandum sive in cæsura
ligni. Unamquisque autem de servis de sua huba debet mittere
in silvam porcos 5. . . Hæc omnia de jure meo in jus et dominium S. Nazarii perpetualiter possidendum."

limited use of the forest; but this right of use is only granted them by the favour of the proprietor, and it is a sort of accessory to the holding which they have received from him. He gives away the whole domain, including the forest and including the serfs; but it is understood that the serfs under the new proprietor shall continue in their holdings and in the enjoyment of their very limited rights to the use of the forest.

Sometimes the owner of the estate divides the forest into two, keeps one part for himself and leaves the other for the use of his tenants.[1] Sometimes, again, he exacts payment in return for these advantages, and this forms part of the yearly rent.[2] Instances of this kind make it clear that the common occupation of a part of a forest does not come down from an earlier custom of joint-ownership, but is connected with the old system of the private estate and its servile holdings.

This brings us to the *allmend.* According to Maurer and his followers, *allmend* is the land common to all; and they say that at first all land was *allmend.* But, in the first place, *allmend* is not to be found in

---

[1] Example in Lacomblet, vol. ii., p. 42.

[2] *Ibidem*: "Homines . . . ex communione silvæ . . . persolvunt censum 32 denariorum. Homines in hac silva communionem habentes persolvunt tres modios avenæ. Homines de communi silva quam vocant Holzmarca persolvunt curti adjacenti duos modios avenæ."

documents earlier than the beginning of the thirteenth
century; and secondly, the word means no more than
the woodland and pasture over which the peasants
had common rights.

The "commons," which are frequently to be met
with in early documents, are the same thing. Mention
is made of them in a Merovingian diploma of 657
(Pardessus, No. 408, Pertz, No. 56); in three charters in
the chartulary of St. Bertin in the eighth century; In
seven formulas and in miscellaneous documents to be
found in various collections of *Traditiones*.[1] Now, it
is easy to see that in all these instances, without a
single exception so far as has yet been found, the
"commons" are spoken of as given, sold, or ex-
changed by some one to whom they belong. The
commons, therefore, are by no means the collective
property of a group of cultivators of the soil. They
form part of a villa, that is of a large estate; and
when this is sold, given away or bequeathed by the
owner, he mentions, in accordance with the usual
practice, the different sorts of land which go to make
up the whole estate; as, for instance, " I, so and so,
give to my nephews the property I possess in such
and such a district, which comprises so many mansi
with buildings, lands, forests, fields, meadows, pastures

[1] Lacomblet, *Urk. für die Gesch. des Niederrheins*, No. 3, anno
793. Zeuss, *Trad.* Wizenburgenses, No. 200. Beyer, *Urkundenbuch zur Gesch. der Mittelrheinischen Territorien*, No. 10,
anno 806.

communia, all the serfs dwelling there, and all that I possess and hold."[1] These commons, which are the property of a single owner, cannot be common to others except so far as the enjoyment of them is concerned, and that only with the goodwill of the owner. As far as we can see, they were that part of the domain which, not being fit for cultivation, was not let out to individual tenants, but left to the tenants to use in common to pasture their animals upon, or for getting wood. But they did not for that reason cease to be the private property of the owner of the estate, who sells them or gives them away precisely like any other part.

These documents of the eighth and ninth centuries, which speak of *communia*, are followed by documents in succeeding centuries which speak of the *allmende*. The two words are the equivalents one for the other, and mean the same thing. The following is an example.

One of the most important documents instanced by Maurer is a deed of the year 1150, in which mention is made of a forest called *allmend*, " where the peasants often go and which is common to them." To

---

[1] *Formulæ*, ed. Rozière, No. 172, ed. Zeumer, p. 276 : "Dulcissimis nepotibus meis . . . dono rem meam, id est, mansos tantos cum ædificiis, una cum terris, silvis, campis, pratis, pascuis, communiis, mancipiis ibidem commanentibus, et quidquid in ipso loco mea est possessio vel dominatio." The word *dominatio*, which is found more than 500 times in charters, has never any other sense than private property, *dominium*.

judge from this phrase, apart from its context, we might
suppose that we have here to do with a mark, that is
to say, with land owned in common by a group of
cultivators. But if we read the whole document we
find that it is a case where an entire villa belongs to
three brothers " by inheritance from their ancestors ; "
that they are making a gift of it to a monastery,[1] and
at the same time transferring their rights over a forest
adjoining the domain. " This forest," they say, " called
in the vulgar tongue *allmend,* is frequented by the
peasants, and is used in common by them and us."[2] But
these peasants are their tenants ; though free in 1150,
they had once been the *coloni,* serfs or *villani* of the
proprietor ; and what proves this is that the authors
of the deed from which we are quoting, add that one of
their ancestors granted these men " civil rights " and
a charter ; and they take care to insert this charter in
the deed so that it may be respected by the new owner.[3]
Here, then, is an instance in which peasants have certain

---

[1] In Wurdtwein, *Nova subsidia diplomatica,* vol. xii, p. 88 :
" Traditionem fundum Uterinae vallis . . . quem habemus a
progenitoribus." This *fundus* has well-marked bounds, and the
charter mentions them all. " His terminis fundus tenetur
inclusus, certis indiciis designatur."

[2] " Silva quaeque adjacentia eidem fundo, quae vulgari lingua
almenda nominatur, quam rustici frequentant, quae juris nostri
sicut et illorum esse dinoscitur communisne ad omnem
utilitatem. . . ."

[3] " Jura etiam civilia eidem fundo competentia, a progenitoribus nostris tradita, huic cartae dignum duximus inserenda, ne
forte succedente tempore excidant a memoria."

rights of use over a forest, but rights which are assuredly not derived from a time when these men were owners of the forest. Some generations before, the whole domain had belonged to a single owner and these people had been his servants; they enjoyed certain rights in the forest as tenants, and these were left to them when they became free men.[1]

What strikes one with astonishment in the writings of Maurer and his disciples is that they omit and leave altogether out of sight a fact which is of vital importance and rests on abundant evidence: the existence of great estates in the early centuries of the Middle Ages. They disregard also the existence of *coloni* and of slaves. But these were to be found not only in Gaul, but even in Germany. Tacitus himself describes the cultivation of the soil in Germany by serfs.[2] He gives a picture of a society full of inequalities, including rich and poor, nobles and simple freemen, freedmen and slaves; and he remarks this peculiar characteristic, that the Germans—those of them who were free, that is—did not themselves cultivate their land, but left the work " to the

[1] The same position of affairs is found in a document of 1279, in Wurdtwein, *ibidem*, p. 218, which Maurer cites, without mentioning that it refers to an arrangement between an abbot and his *villani*.

[2] Tacitus, *Germania*, 25 : " Servis . . . frumenti modum dominus aut pecoris aut vestis, ut colono, injungit ; et servus hactenus paret.

weakest of their slaves."[1]   Later on we see in the laws
of the Burgundians that proprietors of land have
coloni to cultivate their estates;[2] they have slaves;[3]
they have on each estate a manager, *actor*, or a farmer,
conductor.[4]   When the Burgundian king makes a
present to one of his warriors, it is not a small field
that he gives him, but "an estate with its slaves."[5]
The laws of the Alamanni also indicate the existence
of large estates. As to those belonging to the king and
the church the laws give particularly clear information, and show that they were cultivated by slaves,
or by *coloni* who paid a yearly rent in produce or
labour.[6] We may suppose that lands of the same
character were also in the hands of private persons;
for reference is made to their slaves, and in such a
way as to show that they were numerous.[7] Moreover,
the laws speak of slaves holding portions of land,

[1] Tacitus, *Germania*, 15 : " Delegata domus et penatium et
agrorum cura feminis senibusque et infirmissimo cuique ex
familia. Ipsi hebent."   In Latin *familia* means the whole
body of slaves belonging to one man.

[2] *Lex Burgund.*, 68 : "Quicumque agrum aut colonicas tenent."

[3] *Ibidem*, 38, 10 : " De Burgundionum colonis et servis."

[4] *Ibidem*, 50, 5 : " Si privati hominis actorem occiderit."
38, 9 : " Si in villa conductor. . . ."

[5] *Ibidem*, 55 : "Quicumque agrum cum mancipiis largitione
nostra percepit."

[6] *Lex Alamann.*, *partus*, 8, 19, 20, 21 ; *lex*, 22-23.

[7] *Ibid.*, 79 : edit. Lehmann, pp. 138-139. " Si pastor porcarum
. . . Si pastor ovium qui 80 capita in grege habet domini sui . .
Si seniscalcus qui servus est et dominus ejus 12 vaccas infra
domum habet. . . Si mariscalcus qui super 12 caballos est."

with house, stable and barn,[1] by the side of the house
and barn of the owner.[2] In the laws of the Bavarians,
the same classes of *coloni* and slaves make their appearance. Amongst the Thuringians, Frisians and Saxons,
there are slaves and *liti ;* and neither of these classes
is quick to disappear, for they are still to be found in
the documents of the Middle Ages, and to be found
cultivating holdings which belong to an owner and for
which they pay dues.[3] It is also noticeable in the
greater part of these documents, that the owner declares that, in giving or selling his land, he gives or
sells at the same time the slaves, freedmen, *coloni,*
liti ; in a word, all who actually worked on the land.[4]
The number of slaves is considerable.   Thus in a

[1] *Lex. Alam.*, 81, edit. Lehmann, 77, p. 141 : " Si servi
domum incenderit . . . scuriam vel graneam servi si incenderit."

[2] *Ibidem*, art. 4 (6) : "Si spicariam servi incenderit, 3 solidis ;
et si domini, sex solidis."

[3] See, for example, a document of 797 in Lacomblet, No. 9 :
"Dono . . . unam hovam quam proserviunt liti mei ; No. 4 :
terram quam Landulfus litus meus incolebat et proserviebat."
[As to the *liti,* see also Fustel de Coulanges, *L'Alleu,* p. 342, and
Schmid, *Gesetze der Angelsachsen,* pp. 5 (Aethelbirht, 26), 409
(Formula).]

[4] The usual formula runs : " Dono curtem cum domibus acco-
labus, mancipiis, vineis, campis, silvis, etc." Lacomblet, No. 1
et seq. ; Meichelbeck, pp. 27, 34, 36, 49, 51, etc. ; Neugart,
passim. *Laureshamensis,* No. 1 : " Villam nostram cum omni
integritate sua, terris, domibus, litis, libertis, conlibertis, mancipiis." *Monumenta Boica,* viii. 365: "Colonos seu tributales;"
xi. pp. 14 et 15 : " Dedit mansos 26 et vineas cum cultoribus
suis." Zeuss, No. 21 : " villam . . . cum hominibus commanentibus." Zeuss, 36 : " Ipsi servi qui ipsas hobas tenent."

deed of 863, Anafrid makes a grant of an estate and
sixty-four slaves.[1] In 786, Warinus presents the
Abbey of Fulde with a *marca*, which contains thirty
hubs and three hundred and thirty slaves.[2] Some
one else, in 787, gives the lands that he owns in the
marca of Wangheim, and, at the same time, the sixty-
two slaves who cultivate them.[3] Walafrid, in another
marca, gives twenty-eight slaves.[4] In 815, we find a
man of middle rank possessing seven *marsei* and five-
and-twenty slaves.[5] From all this the conclusion is
inevitable that the *marca* or *villa* is an area belonging to one or more proprietors and cultivated by a
much larger number of slaves or serfs—*mancipia, liti,
coloni.*

Maurer would have done better if, instead of devoting so much ingenuity to discovering in the collections
of *Traditiones* a few passages in support of his theory,
he had noticed the evidence which is presented, not in
a few scattered lines, but in every page and in every document, as to the way in which the land was actually distributed. As each document mentions where the landed
property given or sold is situated, we are able to gather
that the geographical unit is the *pagus*, and the rural
unit the *villa*, sometimes called the *marca*. The custo-

[1] *Codex Laureshamensis*, No. 33.
[2] Dronke, *Codex Fuldensis*, No. 84.
[3] *Ibidem*, No. 88.   [4] *Ibidem*, No. 163.
[5] *Codex Laureshamensis*, No. 105. Cf. *Zeuss*, No. 95, where
an owner sells an estate with twenty-two slaves, whose names
he gives.

mary form is: *res sitas in pago N, in villa quæ dicitur N.* The word *villa* is the same word as wo find used in Gaul to designate an estate; the word *marca* which takes its place in about one out of every eight instances, is but its synonym. Sometimes the villa belongs to a single owner, sometimes it is divided amongst several. But, in the one case as in the other, it preserves its earlier unity. The land within it falls into two classes, a *dominicum* and several *mansi*. The *dominicum* or *curtis dominicata* or *mansus dominicatus* is the portion that the owner has reserved for his own use; the other *mansi* or *hubæ*, are the tenant-holdings which he has put into the hands of his *coloni* or his serfs. To take an example. Ansfrid in 863 was owner of the villa of Geizefurt, which comprised a *dominicum* of three *mansi* together with nineteen servile *mansi*.[1] In 868 the *marca* of Gozbotsheim had a *dominicum* of three *mansi*, seventeen servile *mansi*, and serfs to the number of a hundred and forty-six.[2] In 989 a woman represents herself as owning in the marca of Schaffenheim 4 *hubæ dominicales*, 8 *hubæ serviles*, 5 *mansi*, vineyards, meadowland, woodland and a mill, to all which are attached thirty slaves.[3] The *dominicum* is described in the same way in many other documents.[4] Maurer

[1] *Codex Laureshamensis*, No. 33.
[2] *Ibidem*, No. 37.
[3] *Ibidem*, No. 83.
[4] Thus in the villa Frankenheim there is a *curtile dominica-*

supposes (p. 137) that this expression refers to all
that part of the ancient common mark which has become private property. This is a mistake. The
dominicum is the land that the proprietor has not
entrusted to tenants.[1] Wherever we find the *dominicum*, it is an unmistakable sign of a large private estate.
A *dominicum* necessarily implies a lord and his serfs or
coloni. With time the interior organisation of the
villa is modified; it is split up as a consequence of
inheritance and sale, and so we see proprietors owning
not more than four or two *mansi*, or perhaps only one.
Many of the peasants may also have become free
men. But the *dominicum* is still there and bears
witness that in an earlier age the *villa* or *marca* had
a single owner who stood out above a numerous body
of serfs. Maurer pays no attention to all these facts;
he suppresses them, and in their stead conjures up a
picture of mark associates.

Imm, Zeuss, *Traditiones Wizemb.*, No. 127 ; in the villa Caxfelden
a *terra indominicata*, ibid., No. 3 ; in the villa Oterefheim a
curtile indominicatum, ibid., No. 19 ; in the villa or marca
Bruningadurf, a *curtis indominicata*, comprising houses, stables
and barns, and having attached to it about 100 acres in
meadows, fields, vineyards, and woods, *ibidem*, No. 25.

[1] The *dominicum* is mentioned in the laws of the Alamanni,
22 : "servi faciant tres dies sibi et tres in dominico ;" and in the
law of the Bavarians, 1, 14 : "servus tres dies in hebdomada
in dominico operetur, tres vero sibi faciat." It is generally
known that it was the almost universal practice for the dominicum to be tilled and reaped by the tenants.

His theory once set up, he wrests the meaning of documents so that they shall agree with it. Seeing, for instance, in the laws of the Burgundians that the King Gondebaut commands "all his subjects" to observe a law, *universitatem convenit observare*, he believes that the word *universitas* here relates to a village community:[1] and it does not occur to him that this is the usual formula by which the king addresses the whole body of his people. If he sees in the laws of the Visigoths that when any one wishes to change or restore the boundaries of a property, he must do it publicly, in the presence of neighbours, this natural custom becomes in his eyes a right of joint ownership possessed by the neighbours over the land in question.[2] Because some forests are common to several owners, he concludes that all forests are common to all. He maintains that the right of chase belonged to all; and when you examine the authorities from which he draws this conclusion, you discover that he quotes only two, and that these, on the contrary, severely punish the man who has stolen game.[3] Wherever he turns, he

---

[1] Maurer, *Einleitung*, p. 138. *Lex Burgundionum*, xlix. 3 : "Quod prius statutum est, universitatem convenit observare." Cf. the frequent phrase : "noverit universitas fidelium nostrorum."

[2] *Lex Wisigothorum*, x. 3, 2.

[3] Salic law, 33 ; Ripuarian law, 42. Cf. the anecdote told by Gregory of Tours, *Hist.*, x. 10, which is the opposite of what Maurer here maintains.

——— —— —

was the mark. If the King Childebert speaks of the
centena, the *centena* must be the *mark*[1] The duty
of furnishing the king's agents with a lodging when
they are travelling falls on the *mark*[2] If later on
you see a church in every village, it is because, in
times even earlier than Christianity, " the association
of the mark was united by religious bonds;" and in
proof of this he quotes a document of the year 1270
after Christ![3] The "associat's of the mark," he says
again, "are bound to support one another" (page 161),
and the only reference he gives is to the laws of the
Alamanni; you turn to the place indicated, and all
you see there is that two men have a quarrel, that
one of them kills the other, and that the friends of
the victim pursue the murderer.[4] What connection
has this with an association of the mark? The
village, according to him, formed a free self-governing
body, under its own head; and he then instances
the *common loci* of the laws of the Burgundians,[5] though

[1] Maurer, *Einleitung*, p. 164.

[2] *Ibid.*, pp. 165-166.

[3] *Ibid.*, p. 167.

[4] *Les Alamans.*, xlv. Pertz, p. 60 ; edit. Lehmann, pp. 104-
105. It is the word *pares* which deceives him. He believes he
sees in this word the "markgenossen"; but *pares* means the com-
panions, the friends, those who have adopted the cause of one or
other of the adversaries. Similarly article 95 of the same law
punishes the man who, while with the army, deserts *parem
suum*, i.e., his comrade in the battle.

[5] Maurer, p. 140.—Cf. *Leg Burgund.*, xlix. 1: "honores
comites atque praepositi."

it is certain that the *comes*, far from being a village chief, was the royal agent who administered a *civitas*. He does not fail to seize upon the *tunginus* as a chief elected by the villagers; which, again, is pure imagination. He even discovers in a formula of Marculf a *senior communiæ*, "a head of the rural community;" but the passage in Marculf has a totally different meaning. The document in question is a letter written in the name of a certain city begging the king to appoint a bishop, and the expression *seniori communi* is in the heading, amongst the titles given to the king himself. It is a strange mistake to suppose it referred to the principal man of a village community.[1] These members of the village, he goes on to say, had their assemblies (page 141); but for this he produces no authority. "They administered justice amongst themselves;" but how does he explain the fact that there is not a single document to be found referring to such an administration of justice? What we do, on the contrary, frequently find is, that men belonging to a villa or mark are under the jurisdiction of

---

[1] Maurer, p. 140. Marculf. i, 7: "Consensus civium pro episcopatu. Piissimo ac precellentissimo domno illo rege (regi) vel, (remember that *rel* meant *and*) seniori commune illo." *Commune* is for *communi*; and the meaning of the whole is, "To our most pious and excellent king, chief of all the land." The words which follow show clearly that the letter is addressed to the king. "Principalis vestræ clementia novit .... etc., suppliciter postulamus ut instituere dignetis inlustrem virum illum cathedræ illius successorem."

the proprietor or his representative, his *judex*. To
tell the truth, the *communitas* in the sense of a
group of peasants, does not make its appearance until
the thirteenth century.[1] Then only, or a little earlier, do
the inhabitants of the villa or mark act together as a
sort of association for the common enjoyment of
certain privileges. Nothing of the kind appears in
the early part of the Middle Ages.

The success, therefore, of Maurer's theory is not to
be attributed to the strength of his evidence. He
has not furnished us with a single proof, a single
quotation, in support of the community or association
of the mark that he pictures to himself as existing
when history first begins. Go over the innumerable
quotations at the bottom of the pages of his book:
more than two-thirds relate to private property;
of the rest some hundreds are concerned with minor
points unconnected with the subject; not a single
one touches the main question; or if there are any
which at first sight appear to do so, the slightest examination shows that they have been misunderstood and
misinterpreted. The book, nevertheless, has had an
enormous influence. It has won many by its neat
consistency, others by its apparent learning. Any-

---

[1] Documents of 1279 and 1290 in Wurdtwein, *Nova subsidia*,
xii. 218 and 261: "pratum spectans ad Almeindam nostrae
communitatis." Document of 1231 in Guden, *Codex dipl.*, iii.
p. 1102: "contulerunt pascua communitatis quae vulgariter
Almeina vocantur."

thing like verification of its arguments was gladly
dispensed with; especially as this is not an easy
thing to do unless you happen to possess the
originals. And so, year after year, for forty years, the
same story has been repeated, the same arguments
brought forward, the same authorities quoted.

I shall not pursue this theory of Maurer's through
the works of all his disciples; but I ought at least to
notice in passing the latest of them. Dr. K. Lamprecht
has published recently a ponderous and learned work
upon the economic life of Germany in the Middle Ages.[1]
His first volume is a description of the rural economy
of the basin of the Moselle, and his principal object
of study is Frank life in this district. Unfortunately, under the influence of the ideas which have
been dominant in history since the time of Maurer, he
takes as his starting point "the association of
the mark," the *Markgenossenschaft.* "The Frank
people," he says, "grew out of the mark-association;
and that institution has had an influence on the
Frank constitution that cannot be overlooked" (p. 51,
cf. p. 42). Yet he brings forward absolutely no proof,
no indication of this primitive community of the
mark, and gives us nothing but the bare assertion.

He says (p. 46) that the mark appears in Frank
law as an area of land held in common; but he

---

[1] Karl Lamprecht, *Deutsches Wirthschaftsleben im Mittelalter,*
Leipzig, 1886. [Summary in *Zeitsch. f.d. gesante Staatswissen-
schaft,* XLVI., 527 seq.]

does not give a single quotation in which the mark means an area of common land, and it is certain he could not produce one. He tells us that he has seen the *marca* in Ripuarian law, but he neglects to say that this *marca* is the boundary of a private estate, and therefore exactly the opposite of common land.[1] He also mentions that the word occurs again in an edict of Chilperic, and he omits to add that the word *marca* was only introduced into this edict by a conjecture of Professor Sohm's, and that in any case it is impossible to give it in this place the meaning of common land.[2]

"The Frank village," he says, "was a portion of the mark, and the mark was the common property of all its inhabitants; everything was in common—arable land, meadows, forests."[3] You look at the foot of the page for the authorities on which this statement is based, and you find a reference to a document of 786; you turn to this; it is in Beyer, (*Urkundenbuch zur Geschichte der Mittelrheins*, vol. i. p. 19), and you see that it has nothing whatever to do with the mark, that not even the word is to be found in it, and that the document merely relates to a "villa Sentiacus."

The absence of the term *mark*, and of all other like

[1] *Lex Ripuaria*, lx. 5; cf. lxxv.
[2] *Edictum Chilperici*, 8.
[3] K. Lamprecht, *Wirthschaft und Recht der Franken zur Zeit der Volksrechte*, in the *Historisches Taschenbuch*, 1883, p. 57.

terms, from the Franconian laws, does not trouble our author. He discovers there the word *vicini.* To every one else this word signifies *neighbours;* and it is easy to see that every system of law must pay some slight attention to the mutual relations of persons who live near tog ther. In the eyes of Dr. Lamprecht, however, *vicini* stands for *associates;* neighbourhood and common mark are with him one and the same thing. You have neighbours; therefore you form with them part of an association; therefore the land is common to you and to them : such is his process of reasoning. It would greatly surprise one of our peasants of to-day; they are by no means accustomed to identify neighbourhood and corporate union. But a scholar with a theory does not stoop to such small considerations as this. Perhaps, however, some document has come down to us from the Frank period, which would suggest that the men of that time saw a connection between the two things ? Not at all ; not a single clause in a law, not a charter, not a document of any kind suggests that the idea of association was connected with that of neighbourhood. The *vicini* of the Salic law are neighbours in the ordinary sense of the word. But Dr. Lamprecht has a peculiar method of interpreting authorities. There is a certain Merovingian capitulary which runs as follows: " If a man has been killed between two neighbouring *villae,* without its being known who is the murderer,

the count must proceed to the place, call together the
neighbours (that is to say, the inhabitants of the two
neighbouring *villae*) to the sound of the trumpet, and
summon them to appear before his tribunal on an appointed day, for the purpose of declaring on oath that
they are innocent of the murder." The passage is
quite clear, and the method of procedure very natural.
But to Dr. Lamprecht it means that the men were
" associates of the mark " (p. 13, n. 3), and that they
lived in a condition of community. On this he builds
up a complete theory of " neighbourhood," *Nachbar-
schaft*, and he maintains " that this ' neighbourhood ' is
one of the principal factors of the Frank organisation "
(p. 19).

He comes upon this word *vicini*, again, in an edict
of Chilperic. The fact is that this edict declares, 1st,
that land shall continue to pass from father to son in
accordance with the old rule ; 2nd, that in default of
a son the daughter shall inherit; 3rd, that in default of
son and daughter, the collateral relations shall take
the land and the neighbours shall not take it.[1] This
Dr. Lamprecht interprets as if it said that in case
of the failure of the direct line the neighbours formerly
had the right of taking the land ; but the edict of

[1] *Edictum Chilperici*, art. 3: " Filii terram habeant sicut et
hus antea habet ; et filii defuncti fuerint, filia accipiat terras . . . Et
si moritur, frater terras accipiat, non vicini. Et si frater moriens
non fuerit superstitem, tunc soror ad ipsa terra accedat
possidenda."

F.

Chilperic does not say this, and the opposite is positively proved by the section on succession (tit. xli.) in the Salic law. Then, starting with this misinterpretation, he goes on to maintain that the *vicini* had a common right to the land, and were, so to speak, the joint-owners of it; a state of things of which there is not the slightest trace in the documents.

He finds the word *vicini* again in section xlv. of the Salic law, and at once believes that he has discovered a community, and a community of such a kind that it has the right of excluding every new-comer; so that a man who has obtained a field by purchase or bequest has not the right to occupy it without the leave of all the inhabitants. But read this section xlv. and you will see at once that it does not apply to a man who has got a field by lawful means.[1] You will notice, moreover, if you read the entire section—people are always careful not to quote more than a fragment—that there is no mention of any community. Not a single word throughout these twenty-two lines means or suggests the idea of a community or an association.[2] You do not see a body of inhabitants meeting, deliberating, deciding.

---

[1] This is expressed by the words *super alterum*, which mean, "on another man's land." It is also expressed by the heading in more than half the MSS., *de eo qui villam alterius occupaverit*.

[2] It is puerile to maintain that *si unus vel aliqui qui in villa consistunt* means a village community. Where, then, is the word which does mean community?

What you do see is a man, who, in his own name, enters a complaint before the royal functionary, the count, against a certain person who has taken possession of a piece of land, without any right to it; and the count expels the intruder, not in virtue of the rights of the community—not a word of that—but simply in virtue of the rights of private [property, and because the intruder cannot justify his possession by any legitimate title. Where do you find in all this the action of a village community, of an association of the mark? If you think you see it, it is assuredly not because it is in the original, but because your preconceptions have put it there. We have here one of the most striking examples of the result of the subjective method. Your theory requires that a village community should be mentioned in some early document, and you introduce the community into a document where there is nothing about it. And still the mistake might easily have been avoided; for we possess upon this very section xlv. a commentary which was written in 819, and written not by some chance person, but by the counsellors of Louis the Pious.[1] Now these men, who were most of them judges, who consequently were in the habit of administering this law and ought to have known its meaning, saw in it simply this: that if a stranger came and settled himself without a title on land

[1] Pertz, i. 226; Behrend, p. 113, art. 9.

which did not belong to him,[1] it needed only that a
single inhabitant should inform the count, and he would
put an end to the usurpation. But as there was a
final c'ause to the effect that this work of giving
information ought to be performed within twelve
months, and that, at the expiration of that term, the
intruder could remain on the land and enjoy it in
security,[2] the men of 819 demanded that this last
clause should be abrogated.[3] Nothing could be
plainer than the whole affair in the eyes of every one
not under the influence of a preconceived idea. But
Professor Lamprecht chooses to suppose that " the men
of 819 did not understand this document" (p. 47). This
is an easy way out of the difficulty ; to understand a
document otherwise than Professor Lamprecht understands it, is to misunderstand it. It is not possible,
however, to overlook the fact that these counsellors
of Louis the Pious were learned men, who spent half
their lives in deciding cases of law. It must also be
remembered that article xlv. occurs in the law as
amended by Charles the Great; and that whatever
was its original source, it was still a part of the exist-

---

[1] " De eo qui villam alterius occupaverit."

[2] " Si infra 12 menses nullus testatus fuerit, securus sicut et
alii vicini maneat."

[3] " De hoc capitulo judicaverunt ut nullus villam aut res
alterius migrandi gratia per annos tenere possit, sed in quacum-
que die invasor illarum rerum interpellatus fuerit, aut easdem
res quærenti reddat aut eas si potest juxta legem se defendendo
sibi vindicet."

ing law and actually in force. Copied, as it had been, by the counsellors of Charles, how can it be supposed that it was not intelligible to his son's counsellors? I confess that, for my own part, I would rather understand it as it was understood by the men of 819 than as it is understood by Professor Lamprecht. I would rather translate it literally in all its simplicity than put a village community into it, which is not otherwise to be found there.

Professor Lamprecht cannot deny that the Salic law mentions enclosures round corn-fields, meadows, and vineyards, and that this is an indication of private property. According to him, it was the kings who altered the old condition of things and introduced these novelties. But this is mere hypothesis. He maintains that the forest and meadowland at any rate continued to be common, and refers to article 27 of the Salic law. You turn to the passage quoted, believing you will there find a mention of a common forest, a forest where all are free to take wood. You find exactly the contrary: "If any one has taken wood from the forest of another, he shall pay a fine of three *solidi*.[1] This, then, is a forest which is someone's private property, a forest wherein

---

[1] *Lex Salica*, xxvii. 18, ed. Behrend : *Si quis lignu alienu in silva alienu furaverit, solidos 3 culpabilis judicetur.* This is the reading of the Paris MS. 4404. MS. 9653 runs : *Si quis lignu in silva alienu furaverit, solidos 45 culpabilis judicetur.* MS. 4627 runs : *in silva alterius.*

none besides the owner has any rights. But Dr. Lamprecht is not troubled by this. According to him, the
words *silva aliena* mean a common forest. But what
should lead him to attribute this unusual meaning to
the words ? " Because," says he, " in the Salic law
the word *silva* is always used in the sense of
common forest" (p. 48). But the word *silva*
occurs nowhere else except in this section. He then
translates *aliena* as if it signified " foreign." Here
we have, indeed, to do with a word which recurs
as often as thirty-one times in Salic law; but in
each of these thirty-one cases its meaning is unmistakably " belonging to another." The law, for
instance, speaks of *messis aliena, sepem alienam,
hortum alienum, vinea aliena, servus alienus, litum
alienum, caballus alienus, sponsa aliena, uxor
aliena.* The word is always synonymous with
alterius, which is often found taking its place ; and
these very words *silva aliena* are replaced in several
manuscripts by the words *silva alterius.*[1] We must also
notice that the whole of this section 27 concerns theft
committed " in the field of another," " in the garden
of another," "in the vineyard of another," and, finally,
" in the forest of another." Doubt is impossible. In
every case it is a matter of private property ; and the
law uses precisely the same expressions about a forest

[1] *In silva alterius,* MSS. Paris 4627, Montpellier 136, Saint-
Gall 731, Paris 4626, etc.

as about a vineyard or garden. Professor Lamprecht's reading of the passage is opposed to all the evidence. But it was necessary for his argument that the forests should be common; he was only able to find a single section of the law which bore upon forests, and, although this section related to a forest belonging to a single owner, he could not refrain from making use of it; and so he maintains that *silva aliena* means exactly the opposite of what it does mean.

Again, Professor Lamprecht says (p. 46) that "the meadows were common," although nothing of the kind is mentioned in the Salic law or in any other document. More than that, if it is in a fact that the meadows were common according to the Salic law, how is it that only once in the Salic law is any reference made to meadows, and then only to punish with the enormously heavy fine of 1500 denarii the person who takes a cartload of hay from another man's field (tit. xxvii, sections 10 and 11)? Professor Lamprecht also maintains that mills were common, although the law only mentions mills belonging to private owners. He fastens on authorities which are absolutely opposed to his theory, and then interprets them according to his liking. If, for instance, he sees that the Salic law punishes severely "anyone who

---

¹ See section xxii. The Munich MS. has in codice aliena. Further on, aratrum is replaced in the Wolfenbüttel MS. by a cui molinum est.

ploughs or sows the field of another without the permission of the owner, *extra consilium domini*," he maintains that this regulation is in his eyes an indication of community in land. If he sees in another place that a man who is unable to pay a fine must swear " that he possesses nothing upon the earth or under the earth ; " this is so much proof that land is not an object of private ownership. The word *facultas* occurs frequently in documents of this period, and it always signifies a man's entire property, real and personal without distinction ;[1] but, as the theory requires that real property should not be too prominent in Salic law, Professor Lamprecht supposes that the word applies only to personal property.

Such is the character of the method he follows. By the aid of such so-called scholarship everything is to be traced back to a primitive community. Although the Frank documents of the Merovingian and Carlovingian periods make no mention of such a community, although they show exactly the opposite ; the whole rural organisation, the entire social life must be the outgrowth of this community of the *mark*. "The *mark* is the foundation, *substratum*, of everything" (p. 282). An infallible rule is supposed to have been found ; and the whole history of the Middle Ages, willy nilly, must be made to fit into it.

---

[1] See the *Formulæ* of *Marculfus* I. 35 ; II. 8 ; *Andegarenses*, 36 (37) ; Rozière, No. 252 ; *Turonenses*, 17.

II.

M. Viollet's theory as to community of land amongst the Greeks.

M. Viollet is a disciple of Maurer who copies and exaggerates his master. The system that Maurer was able with some show of probability to build up in relation to the Germanic peoples, M. Viollet supposes he can extend to all nations ancient or modern. What is quite fresh in his writings and exclusively his own, is, that he attributes to the ancient Greeks a system of community in land which the most profound students of Greek history had, up to this time, failed to discover. We must not suppose that in laying down such a proposition, he is speaking of some primitive age when the Greeks may be supposed to have been ignorant of agriculture, and consequently of landed property. He is speaking of the times when the Greeks were agriculturists, when they lived in organised societies; he is speaking of Greek cities; and he declares that the soil was for a long time cultivated by the city in common, without its occurring to the family or the individual to appropriate it. All the land, according to him, for a long time belonged not to the individual, not to the family, but to the city.[1]

He states that "his theory is supported by authorities of considerable weight" (p. 463); and he refers to eleven passages taken from Plato, Virgil, Justin, Tibullus, Diodorus on the Lipari Isles, Diogenes Laertius on Pythagoras, Aristotle on the town of Tarentum, Athenæus on Spartan meals, Diodorus on the "klerouchia," and lastly, Theophrastus on the sale of real property. Let us look at the originals. Let us see at anyrate whether M. Viollet's references are altogether exact.

1. The first author quoted is Plato, "who still saw here and there the vestiges of primitive community," and M. Viollet tells us that he finds this in the Laws of Plato (Book III.). I turn to the passage mentioned, and this is what I find: "In very early times men lived in a pastoral state, supporting themselves by their herds of cattle and by hunting. At that time they had no laws. As to government, they knew no other than the δυναστεία, the authority, that is, of the master over his family and slaves. Like the Cyclops of Homer, they had neither public assemblies nor justice; they lived in caverns; and each ruled over his wife and children without troubling himself about his neighbours."

[1] P. Viollet, *Du caractère collectif des premières propriétés immobilières*, in the *Bibliothèque de l'École des Chartes*, 1872, pages 455-504.

This is what Plato says, describing from imagination
a primitive savage state. It must be some strange
illusion which makes M. Viollet suppose that this
passage describes men as cultivating the land in
common. Plato says that they did not cultivate it
at all. Where does he see that the land belonged
to the people? Plato says that at this time
there did not even exist a people. Where does
he see that men were associated for purposes of
cultivation? Plato says that each family lived apart,
" without troubling itself about its neighbours." M.
Viollet then has taken this passage in precisely the
opposite sense to the right one. Go through all the
writings of the philosopher and you will find that he
has nowhere said " that in his time he still saw the
ruins of a primitive community." Plato has, it is true,
endowed his ideal city with a particular system of
community in land; but he never says that it was
practised in any actually existing city. Our first
authority, then, is proved to have been misrepresented.

2. M. Viollet next refers to Virgil, who, in the
Georgics (i. 125), describes a time " when the soil was
neither divided nor marked out by boundaries, and
when everything was common." This at first sight
seems convincing. The poet's verse is correctly
quoted.[1] But observe the context. The whole

---

[1] " Nec signare quidem aut partiri limite campum Fas erat ;
in medium quaerebant." M. Viollet makes a mistake, however,
as to *in medium*, which he translates as if it was *in commune*.

passage is an imaginary description of a time when
men did not cu'tivate the soil: *Ante Jovem nulli
subigebant arva coloni . . . Ipsa tellus omnia liberius,
nullo poscente, ferebat.* So long as men did not cultivate the ground, there could be no question of dividing it among them as private property. Virgil goes
on to say that afterwards man learnt to till the
ground, *ut sulcis frumenti quæreret herbam;* but he
no longer says that everything was in common. It
appears, then, that if M. Viollet had given it a little
more attention, he would have dispensed with the use
of this passage ; for it describes savage life and
has no connection at all with community of land
in the agricultural state. What can the golden
age, whether it existed or not, prove concerning the
social life of Greek cities ?

3. Next comes a quotation from Justin out of Trogus
Pompeius. This Gaul, trying to describe the remotest
ages of Italy, says that there was a time " when slavery
and private property were unknown, and everything
was undivided." The quotation is correct ; but what
is the time referred to ? The age before Jupiter, *ante
Jovem.* This is as much as to say, the golden age, or,
if you prefer it, the savage state.

4. It is the same with the quotation from Tibullus ;
it applies " to the time of King Saturn," that is, to the
præ-agricultural age, the golden age of the imagination. If M. Viollet wished to prove that in the

golden age private property did not exist, he has succeeded pretty well. But what has this to do with the Greek cities? M. Viollet supposes that legends of this kind represent traditions of an earlier state. This is exceedingly doubtful; and in any case they would be traditions of a time when agriculture was unknown, and when there were neither organised nations nor cities. If there were long ages when mankind did not know how to till the ground, what does that prove in relation to the time when they did cultivate it? We must not lose sight of the proposition our author wishes to establish; it is that men, even after they had entered into city life, cultivated the soil in common instead of appropriating it individually. There is a certain want of caution in thinking that you can prove a system of common cultivation from legends which show the absence of all cultivation.

5. M. Viollet at last comes down to historical times and quotes a passage from Diodorus Siculus. Let us first give his translation as if it were scrupulously exact: " Certain Cnidians and Rhodians colonised the Lipari Isles. As they had much to endure at the hands of Tyrrhenian pirates, they armed some barks wherewith to defend themselves, and divided themselves into two separate *classes*; one was intrusted with the cultivation of the islands, which they *declared common property*; to the other was committed the care of the

defence. *Having thus thrown together all their possessions,* and eating together at public meals, they lived
in common during several years; but after a time
they divided amongst themselves the land of Lipara
on which was their town; as to the other islands they
continued for some time to be cultivated in common.
At last they divided all the islands for a period of
twenty years; and at the expiration of this term, they
drew lots for them anew."

Much might be said about this translation, but we
wish to be brief.[1]   M. Viollet ought, in the first place,
to have mentioned the date of this event, since
Diodorus gives it: it happened in the fiftieth Olym-
piad, that is about the year 575. Now, long before
this, Cnidus and Rhodes had had a system of private
property, and had no trace of common ownership.
So these Cnidians and Rhodians may, very likely,
have made an experiment of this kind; but it is impossible that their action should illustrate a survival
of primitive community as M. Viollet maintains.[2]

[1] We have italicised the words that are inexact. Diodorus
does not say that these men were divided into two "classes;" he
does not say that they "declared" the land "common property."
κοίνας ποιήσαντες means that the islands were made common for
a moment, it is the statement of a fact, not the announcement
of a perpetual institution. In place of "they threw together all
their possessions," the Greek tells us that they clubbed together
their resources. However, the chief mistakes are in the last
words of the translation.

[2] Viollet, pp. 467-468.

The account of the Greek historian also plainly shows the motive which determined these men to leave the land for some time undivided: it was because the Tyrrhenian pirates ravaged the islands to such an extent that the Greeks were obliged to separate into two divisions, the one fighting, the other tilling the ground.[1] But Diodorus goes on to say that this manner of life only lasted a few years. So soon as they had freed themselves from the pirates, the Greeks made a regular settlement in the island of Lipara, that is in the largest and most important island of the little group. They built a town there; and at the same time "they made a partition of the soil." Now, this partition was never made over again; it was a distribution of shares to be held in perpetuity, that is, as private property. M. Viollet passes over this too hastily; it is of the utmost importance, for it shows us that private property was established directly the Greeks were in anything like a settled condition. The fact that the other islets, more difficult to cultivate and less securely held, remained for some time longer undivided, does not imply that these people lived in a state of agrarian communism. Each of them was a landed proprietor in the main island, and enjoyed certain rights over one of the islets.[2] But even this arrangement did not

---

[1] The passage is in Diodorus v. 9, bipontine edit., iii. p. 387.

[2] Thucydides explains this very well: "They lived on the

last long, and the small islands were parcelled out in their turn. There was, it is true, a provisional partition at first, to last for twenty years; there are several very likely explanations for this precautionary measure. Whatever the reason may have been, at the end of twenty years the partition was made over again, and this time it was permanent; for Diodorus never says that a division took place periodically down to his own time.[1]

The whole account of the Greek historian points to the fact that the Greek emigrants established what was customary throughout Greece, a system of private ownership. In order to thoroughly understand it, we must compare this with similar passages in which the same historian shows us Greek colonists dividing

island of Lipara, and went from thence to cultivate the other islands," iii. 88.

[1] Τὰς νήσους εἰς εἴκοσι ἔτη διελόμενοι, πάλιν κληρουχοῦσιν ὅταν ὁ χρόνος οὗτος διέλθῃ. The word πάλιν means a second time and not periodically. There is no expression such as νῦν ἔτι which the historian would have used if he had meant to imply that it was still practised in his own time. The conjunction ὅταν indicates a single action; the historian has not written ὁσάκις. It is true he uses κληρουχοῦσι in the present tense; whether copying an old document, or employing the "narrative present" so usual with historians. It is necessary, moreover, to notice the intrinsic meaning of the word κληρουχεῖν; the term is usual enough in Greek for its meaning to be perfectly well ascertained. It is always used of a definitive division, a partition made for all time. We cannot suppose that Diodorus would have used κληρουχεῖν for a temporary and periodical division.

the soil amongst themselves from the very first day of their settlement.[1] The settlement of those Cnidians and Rhodians differs from other instances only in this, that it was necessary, for reasons which Diodorus indicates, to postpone the partition for some years. This is what the historian wished to tell us; he never says that these people thought of establishing common ownership: they had no more disposition for it than other Greeks. Whatever communism they may have practised was not an institution, but a temporary condition of things, lasting for a brief period, with no past and no future. Private property was with them, as with all other Greeks, the normal state of things. The account of Diodorus is, we see, the reverse of M. Viollet's statement; and it is startling to find M. Viollet writing, that " as late as *the time of the Emperor Augustus*, private property was not yet established amongst these Greeks, at the very gates of Rome " (p 468).

6. M. Viollet now passes on to Pythagoras. On the evidence of a biography of the philosopher written eight hundred years after his death, he relates that Pythagoras got together as many as two thousand disciples, and induced them to live in common. This may be true; but does the fact that a philosopher succeeded in founding a phalanstery, which did not outlast himself, prove that it was habitual at

---

[1] Diodorus, v. 53; v. 59; v. 81; v. 83 and 84; xii 11; xv. 92.

that time for people to live together in common ? It
seems to me that it proves exactly the opposite. If
the disciples of Pythagoras were forced to leave their
towns in order to found a communistic settlement, it
was because the life in the towns was not communistic.
It is certain that this institution of Pythagoras was
something exceptional, which left no trace behind it.
The story itself, when we look at it, has no connection with a primitive community in land. But
notice M. Viollet's method of proceeding. Just because he comes across these two thousand (others
say six hundred) disciples of Pythagoras, he concludes that "we have here the origin of many of the
towns in Greater Greece ; this shows that these towns
were founded and settled under a system of undivided property." Nothing of the kind. They
were all founded before Pythagoras, and outlived
him ; and neither before nor after his time did they
recognise a system of undivided property.[1]

7. We now come to an instance which would appear
to be more historical. "The citizens of Tarentum,"
says M. Viollet, "seem to have preserved something
of their old community in land down to the time of
Aristotle." And he refers to the *Politics* vi. 3, 5.
You turn to the passage quoted and you read as
follows : "It is the duty of an intelligent aristocracy
to watch over the poor and to furnish them with em-

---

[1] See Strabo vi. 1.

ployment. We should do well to imitate the men of
Tarentum; they have portions of land whered they
leave to the poor the common enjoyment (literally,
which they make common to the poor for their enjoyment [1]), and in this way they secure the attachment of
the lower people." We see how far removed the
original is from M. Viollet's interpretation of it.
Aristotle says nothing whatever of a communistic
system. He places Tarentum amongst aristocratic
States, and shows that there were poor people, ἄποροι,
in it; only he points out that the rich took care to
set apart certain land *for the use* of these poor, in
order to win their attachment.[2] M. Viollet has
mistaken a charitable institution for a communistic
one, though it is perfectly clear that what Aristotle
describes was merely a concession made by the
rich to the poor; that is to say, it was precisely the
opposite of communism.

8. M. Viollet tells us that there are "other
survivals which enable us to travel back in thought
to primitive common-ownership: there are the common meals;" and he devotes fully three pages to
the common meals of the Greeks. He begins with
the meal which the Spartans called *Copis*; describes it
in detail from Athenæus, and concludes (p. 471): " All
this is primitive, and we have here the common meal

---

[1] Κοινὰ ποιοῦντες τὰ κτήματα τοῖς ἀπόροις ἐπὶ τὴν χρῆσιν.
[2] Εὖνοι παρασκευάζουσι τὸ πλῆθος.

in all its early simplicity." Now, it unluckily happens that the meal called *copis* was in no way a common meal. Ancient writers tell us that the Spartans had some private meals;[1] the *copis* was one of them. Read the page from Athenæus which M. Viollet has translated; read it in the original;[2] and not only will you not find a word which suggests that the copis was a public meal, but you will find clear evidence to the contrary. "Whoever likes gives the copis, κοπίζει ὁ βουλόμενος," and he who gives it invites to it whomsoever he pleases, "whether Spartan or stranger." Such are not the characteristics of public meals ordered and arranged by the State. Let us add that the Greek writer lays stress upon the religious character of this meal; it ought to be celebrated before the god παρὰ τὸν θεὸν, *i.e.*, in front of a temple and in presence of the image of the divinity. Ancient rites are observed; a tent must first be built with branches of trees, and the ground strewn with boughs for the company to recline upon; the only meat which may be used is goats' flesh; and each guest must be pre-

[1] Xenophon *Commentarii*, i. 2, 61, tells us that the Lacedæmonian Lichas was celebrated for the generosity with which he entertained his guests at dinner; Herodotus, vi. 57, represents individuals as inviting a king to dinner in their own houses; Plutarch, *Lycurgus*, 12, says that every Spartan who made a sacrifice was excused from the public meals, *i.e.*, he could eat at his own home the animal he had sacrificed. It is, therefore, a great mistake to say that the Spartans always ate in common.

[2] Athenæus, iv. 16.

sented with a particular kind of loaf, made according
to a fixed rule both as to its ingredients and shape.
These rites will not surprise anyone who is familiar
with early Greek life. Every Spartan could give this
repast when he pleased ; but the usual custom in the
town was to give it " at the festival called Tithenidia,
celebrated to secure the health of children ;" and the
nurses used to bring the little boys to it. The description of Athenæus is perfectly clear. M. Viollet has
committed the error of mistaking a private and religious meal for a common meal, and of supposing that
he sees in it a sign of community in land.

There still remain the true common meals, which
took place daily or almost daily at Sparta, and which
were called συσσίτια. M. Viollet says at once that
they are evidence of community. It seems reason-
able to argue : " If men eat the fruits of the earth
in common, it is because in primitive times the earth
itself was common ;" but we think that M. Viollet
ought to have distrusted this apparently logical process of reasoning. If he had studied this institution
of common meals at Sparta in the original writers, he
could not have failed to notice four circumstances :
1. It does not date from the earliest period of the
city ; and far from being connected with a time when
land may have been common, it is later than the
institution at Sparta of private property.[1] 2. These

[1] Herodotus, who knew Sparta very well, says that the public

common meals did not constitute a common life; for in the first place the men alone partook of them, not the women nor the children;[1] and in the second place, the men did not take all the meals of the day together, but only one, that of the evening. 3. The expenses of the meal were not defrayed by the community, by the State, but each man had to bring his contribution, which was fixed at a *medimnus* of flour a month, eight *congii* of wine, some fruit, and a sum of money for the purchase of meat.[2] This is something very different from citizens being fed in common by the State; they had to eat in common, but each ate at his own expense, because each was the owner of property. 4. The common meals were so far from representing community in goods, that poor Spartans were not admitted to them; a fact which is distinctly mentioned by Aristotle, who goes on to say that these meals were the least democratic things in the world.[3]

It is the greatest mistake to imagine all the Spartans eating of the same dishes at the same table. The

meals were not established till two centuries after the foundation of the city; i. 65. The same will be found in Xenophon, *Republ. Laced.*, v. and in Plutarch, *Lycurgus*, 10, who says distinctly that before this period the Spartans ate their meals at home. Private property, on the other hand, was established from the very beginning of the city.

[1] Plato, *Laws*, vi. p. 781; Aristotle, *Politics*, ii. 7; Alcman, in Strabo, x. 4, 18.

[2] Aristotle, *Politics*, ii. 7; Plutarch, *Lycurgus*, 12.

[3] Aristotle, *Politics*, ii. 6, 21.

so-called common meals were taken in small groups of fifteen members each, in separate houses. Every one was free to choose the group which he wished to join; but he was not admitted except by the unanimous vote of the members composing it.[1] We also know that the meals were somewhat luxurious, and that the famous black broth, μελάς ζωμος, was merely the prelude to them.[2] It is, then, very evident that these common repasts, whose meaning or object we need not here try to discover, have not the slightest connection with a common life and certainly not with community in land.[3]

M. Viollet also refers to the feasts which the fifty Athenian *prytanes* used to celebrate near the sacred hearth; reminds us that when the young Athenian was received into the *phratria*, the *phratria* performed a sacrifice which was followed by a feast; and refers to the feasts which the Roman *curiæ* celebrated before an altar on certain festivals. But one must indeed be dominated by a fixed idea to suppose that these three different kinds of feasts are a proof of community in land. It is exceedingly ingenious to say that

[1] Plutarch, *Lycurgus*, 12.

[2] Cicero, *Tusculan. Disput.* v. 34 ; Plutarch, *Lycurgus*, 21 ; Xenophon, *Republ. Laced.*, v ; and, above all, the authors cited by Athenæus, iv, 20.

[3] We have elsewhere pointed to the evidence for private property in Sparta, and the rules concerning it. (*Comptes rendus des séances de l'Académie des sciences morales*, 1879-1880.) See, on the same subject, the excellent work of M. Claudio Jannet.

" these meals are the lingering evidence of a primitive
nomad life and of community in the soil;"[1] but the fact
is that they were simply religious ceremonies. They
were celebrated around an altar, according to prescribed rites. The custom of a common meal in the
presence of the divinity is found in many religions.

9. For his ninth proof, M. Viollet sets before us
" a wide-spread tradition which represents the inhabitants of a country as dividing its soil amongst
themselves ;" and in support of this he gives a few
references to Diodorus. He might have given many
more, and to other writers also.[2] What he takes for
a vague tradition is an historical fact perfectly well
known and authenticated. We know that every
Greek city preserved the memory of its foundation,
which was the occasion of a yearly festival. This
tradition was handed down either by means of religious songs repeated from year to year without any
change, or on bronze inscriptions kept in a temple.
It is from these sacred records that we obtain such
exact evidence as to the founding and founder of each
city. Now these records lay stress on two circumstances ; the founding of the town on a given day by
the performance of a religious ceremony ; and the
division of the land amongst the citizens,—a division

[1] Viollet, p. 472.

[2] Diodorus, v. 53 ; v. 59 ; v. 81 ; v. 83 ; v. 84 ; xii. 11 ; xv.
23; Odyssy, vi. 11 ; Herodotus, v. 77 ; Plato, *Laws*, iii. pp. 684-
685 ; Pausanias, *passim*.

which was effected by a drawing of lots, called κληρουχία or κλορωσία. These two operations took place at the same time; we might almost say on the same day. Where M. Viollet makes the mistake is in saying that " this division presupposes primitive community, and puts an end to an era of non-division" (p. 473). It is precisely the contrary ; for whenever we see Greek emigrants making settlements on territory either previously unoccupied or else conquered by them, we find them *immediately* founding a town and *immediately* dividing the soil.[1] The soil may have been conquered in common, but not for one single year is it cultivated in common. They do not divide it " in order to get out of a system of non-division"; but they make haste to divide the country that they have just found unoccupied or have just conquered, so that it shall not remain for one moment undivided.

In those cities, indeed, which date from very early times, there was no occasion for a division. We do not find it in Athens. Why? Because we know that Attica was at first occupied by some hundreds of independent families, γένη ; and that these families afterwards were grouped into phratries, and finally into a city. There is no partition here, for each family keeps the land which has belonged to it for centuries.

---

[1] We do not doubt that there were some exceptions. What Diodorus tells us of the Lipari Islands is one of them. It might occasionally sometimes happen, for some reason or other, that the partition was put off for a few years.

But when it is a case of a colony, a body of people who emigrate and take possession of fresh territory, a division is quite needful. Only this division does not, as M. Viollet would suppose, come at the end of a period of non-division; it is the first step in the establishment of the colony. The practice is one of the most re-markable, and one of the best authenticated of those early times. It proves that the Greek city never cultivated its land in common; that it had no wish for a common ownership of the soil; that the very idea of such a system was unknown to it. If M. Viollet had studied the κληρουχία in all the authorities which refer to it, he would not have supposed for a moment that it could be a proof of community in land, and he would have taken care not to bring it forward in support of a theory of which it is in reality the refutation.

10. I shall not dwell long upon another argument of M. Viollet's (p. 481). I have elsewhere pointed out that in the most ancient Greek law, as well as in early Hindoo law and with many other peoples, the land originally attached to a family was so closely bound up with it that it could neither be sold, nor transferred to another family, either by bequest or as dower.[1] This rule is clearly explained in many Greek writings; it is the result of the conception of pro-

[1] Heraclides of Pontus, edit. Didot, vol. ii. p. 211 ; Aristotle, *Politics*, ii. 4, 4 ; vii. 2, 5 ; Plutarch, *Instituta laconica*, 22 ; *Life of Agis*, 5 ; *Life of Solon*, 21. Cf. *Laws of Manou*, ix. 105-107, 125,

perty not as an individual right, but as a family right.
A father was compelled to leave it to his sons. Even
if there were no son, he could not bequeath or sell
it; it must pass to the nearest relation. M. Viollet
imagines that there is another explanation. The
prohibition of sale and bequest results, according
to him, from the circumstance that land was
originally common to all. I do not follow the argument. If the soil was originally the common
property of the people, and the people maintained a
kind of eminent domain over it (which is M. Viollet's
theory), one cannot see why the law should have
forbidden the sale of land to another member of the
same people; one cannot see why the law should
have prohibited any family from parting with it, even
in favour of the people itself. The old rule, or rather
the ancient custom which forbids a family to separate
itself from its land, cannot be a proof of community
in land. It only proves the ownership of property by
the family. As Plato says, in a passage where he
expresses not his own private utopias but the ideas of
the men of his time: "You cannot leave your property
to whomsoever you please, because your property belongs to your family, that is, to your ancestors and
your descendants."[1] The hypothesis that M. Viollet
sets against this is purely fanciful. He appears to
believe that the restriction as to sale and bequest

---

[1] Plato, *Laws*, xi.

weakened the rights of property; he does not observe
that it renders inheritance more absolute, and secures
the rights of the family. One may search through
the whole of Greek law and the whole of Greek
literature without finding either the "eminent domain"
of the State, or a restoration of the land to a supposed
ownership common.

11. M. Viollet's last argument is taken from a
passage of Theophrastus. When Greek law at last
authorised the sale of land—property being from that
time onwards looked upon as an individual right,—it
required that the sale should take place under certain
conditions of publicity. "Many legislators," says
Theophrastus, "require that sales should be made
by a public crier, and that they should be an-
nounced several days beforehand; others prefer that
they should take place in the presence of a magistrate;
while some lay down that notice of sale must be posted
up for sixty days. There are two motives for all this:
in the first place that claims may be presented against
the seller, and secondly, that all may know who is
the new owner." This sentence is perfectly clear; it
tells us that a sale ought to be made publicly, so that
it may be surrounded by all possible guarantees; but
M. Viollet sees in it something different from this.
" If the public are present," he says, " it is because the
land belongs to the people" (pp. 484-485). This is
drawing a conclusion of which Theophrastus never

dreamt. When he described the various kinds of publicity which were enjoined in the matter of sale, and when he explained in such a natural manner the reasons for this publicity, he did not suppose that his meaning would be so far distorted as to lead to the conclusion that the land had once been common. But M. Viollet has a fixed idea and follows it. If he reads that neighbours act as witnesses to a sale, he adds that their consent had doubtless to be asked, since the land properly belonged to all. If he reads in another passage that it was the custom in a certain town for the purchaser to present three of the neighbours with a small piece of money, so that they might afterwards remember the act and be able to vouch for it, he at once adds that " this piece of money is the price which the purchaser pays to the three neighbours for their original rights over the land." All this is pure imagination. The Greeks certainly did not connect any idea of community in land with these simple customs.

Such, then, are the eleven authorities by whose help M. Viollet tries to prove that the early Greek cities held their land in common during a period more or less protracted. M. Viollet does not give a single other reference. Now the first taken from Plato, the fifth from Diodorus, and the seventh about Tarentum are absolutely incorrect ; the second, third and fourth from Virgil, Trogus Pompeius and Tibullus are beside the subject, since they apply to the tradition of a savage state which does not here concern us; the sixth, the one about Pythagoras, points to an exceptional episode, only lasting for a brief period, and clearly not in harmony with Greek habits; the eighth, about public meals, has been misunderstood; the ninth about the κληρουχίαι, and the tenth concerning the primitive inalienability of land belonging to the family, are absolutely opposed to M. Viollet's theory; the eleventh points to publicity of sale, not community in land. And so out of eleven quotations or arguments there is not a single one which on examination stands firm.

And this is not all. Supposing that there could be found in the whole of Greek literature two or three, or even eleven, quotations, which seemed to imply community in land, it would still be the duty of every serious historian to look at the evidence on the other side; to search, that is, for other passages or other facts which point to an opposite conclusion. It did not occur to M. Viollet to do this. If he should ever think of undertaking the task, I venture to point out to him four classes of authorities or of facts: 1st, Those to be found in Homer, Hesiod and the most ancient documents, which show us the land held as private property, with no mention or trace of community. 2nd, Those vestiges of the oldest Greek law which have come down to us, which do not contain the slightest trace of a state of things in which the land belonged to the people, and which do contain, on the contrary, precise rules as to family property. 3rd, The rites of ancient religions, which show the worship of land and of consecrated bounds; and this side by side with the worship of the dead. 4th, and finally, the records of all the κληρουχίαι; that is, the division of the soil into hereditary portions, a division which was made on the very day of the founding of each city, and almost implies an actual inaptitude for common ownership. Here will be found, not eleven imaginary pieces of evidence, but a whole body of evidence and of facts; and this mass of evidence proves precisely the opposite of a system of community. History would be too easy a science if it were enough to pick out here and there isolated lines and interpret them as one liked. *Every* authority ought to be consulted, the *whole* of Greek literature ought to be studied, in treating of such a problem as M. Viollet's. One cannot judge of the whole Greek world from a chance occurrence in the Lipari isles. Eleven quotations, which, even if they were exact, would be insignificant in comparison with the rest of Greek literature, are not enough to build a system upon. What is especially surprising is that the author of such a theory should not have thought of studying either the law, or the beliefs, or the permanent institutions of the Greeks. He has solved the question without so much as setting himself to investigate it.

May I add that I am sorry to find myself taken to

task by M. Viollet? "M. Fustel," he says (p. 464), "was unable to recognise this great historical fact (*i.e.*, the supposed community in land), because he saw that every family had its own hearth, its own worship, its own ancestors." This is true. I willingly grant that the facts which I saw, and which I have completely proved, prevented me from seeing the imaginary facts that M. Viollet thought he descried in his eleven quotations. He further adds (p. 465), that since I admitted the existence of property common to the family, it was an easy thing to go a little further and recognise, as he did, the common-ownership of the people. Here M. Viollet throws a little too much light upon his own method of proceeding. According to him, an historian who recognises one fact or institution ought to guess at another fact or institution, merely because there is an apparent analogy between them; in this way logic takes the place of evidence, and the imagination can construct all the systems it chooses. I am not bold enough for this; I do not find in history what I wish to find, but only what is there. I am careful not to insert anything I do not find. I saw in ancient law and ancient religion the co-proprietorship of the family, and I said so. I did not see the common ownership of the whole people, and I did not say I did. History is not a science of speculation; it is a science of observation.

No one, moreover, but M. Viollet, considers that the

co-proprietorship of the family and the common
ownership of the whole people "are two things which
resemble one another." It is clear to every careful
observer that they are essentially different, both in
character and in results. The co-proprietorship of
the family is an ownership which is complete, absolute, hereditary, independent even of the State. If it
is undivided, it is because the family at this time
is itself still undivided. It is, besides, legally in the
hands of the head of the family, the real owner, who
is absolute master of it, and does what he likes with
it; but who can neither transfer it or bequeath it
" because he owes it to his descendants such as he has
received it from his ancestors." What resemblance is
there between such a system and one under which the
land would be common to all, and belong to a whole
nation ?

I shall not dwell at length on the second portion of
M. Viollet's work, in which he gives a hasty and
superficial glance at the Middle Ages. Here I have
not been more fortunate than before in verifying his
evidence. For example: he dwells at length upon the
prior right of purchase which belonged to neighbours.
Everyone knows of this custom, the meaning and reason of which are obvious enough. But in M. Viollet's
eyes this right of the neighbours is a vestige of community in land. He does not notice that the prefer-
ence given in case of sale to a neighbouring proprietor

G

over a distant one has nothing to do with community.
Under a system of common ownership this prior claim
of the neighbour would not be found.   The two things
are incompatible.   The right of the neighbour is a
custom belonging essentially to private property; it is
a grave error to convert it into a communistic practice.

Further on, M. Viollet speaks of the Franks; he
represents them as "dwelling in small groups called
villæ or *genealogiæ*." One must never have seen in the
charters what a *villa* is, to imagine it a group of men;
and it is something more than rashness to identify
the *villa* with the *genealogia*.   M. Viollet says again
that amongst the Franks " the tie of neighbourhood
was so strong as to hold in check the rights of blood
in matters of succession;" and he does not notice that
this is absolutely opposed to the explicit statement
of the Salic law.   He maintains that the Frank
villa was a village community, and quotes section
xlv. of the Salic law, which not only does not say
one single word about a community, but, on the contrary, one is surprised to find, has nothing whatever to do with one.   He maintains that the Ripuarian law requires " the consent of the community "
to a sale of land, and quotes a section of the law
which merely says that the sale ought to take place
in the presence of witnesses and in a public place.   It
is his own addition that these witnesses are " a
community," and that they have to give their " con-

sult." Elsewhere he maintains that the Thuringians were unacquainted with the sale of land, and his only proof is the section of the law which authorises such a sale. He says again that according to the Ripuarian law real property could only be sold by virtue of a royal writ; and he supports this statement by a reference to the section of the law which enacts that the purchaser of an estate shall demand a written document from the seller.

M. Viollet's quotations are always exact in this respect, that the line he quotes is to be found at the place mentioned; their inexactness merely consists in this, that the same line taken with its context means precisely the opposite of what M. Viollet says. In the same way he once quoted a passage from a document of 890 in which he found the word *communes*; surely this meant community in land, collective ownership. Unluckily it turned out that the document did not contain any reference to community, or even to a village, or to cultivators of the soil; it concerned a dispute between two landowners, an abbot and a count. The adjective *communes* related not to lands, but to certain "customary rights in a royal forest." The abbot declared that "these common rights were his," free of charge, while the count maintained that the abbot had always paid a rent, *sub conductione*. All this is evidently the very opposite of community; but M. Viollet had seen the word *communes*, and that was enough.[1] I have gone through his whole work in a similar manner and tried to find a reference that was to the point; and I have not found one.

III.

Mommsen's theory as to community of land amongst the Romans.

One never for a moment expected to find agrarian communism amongst the Romans; in the first place because Rome was one of the youngest of the cities of the ancient world, and, at the date of its birth, private property had long held sway in Italy; and, in the second place, because it is well known that the Romans had a very precise and very firm conception of the right of private property, and did as much as any other ancient people to define and protect it. And yet Professor Mommsen states that with the Romans "land was originally held in common;" that "community in land is closely bound up with the constitution of the city;" that "it was only in later times that the land was divided amongst the citizens

---

[1] The statement of M. Viollet is in the *Revue critique*, 1886, vol. ii., p. 109. The document of 890 ought not to be interpreted from the extract he gives from it; it is necessary to read the whole of it, as it is to be found in the *Urkundenbuch der Abt i S. Gallen*, n° 662, vol. ii., p. 265.

as private property." [1] In support of this assertion,
the learned and able historian gives three references—
to Cicero, Dionysius of Halicarnassus, and Plutarch.
But on examining these three references it seems to
me that none of them says exactly what Professor
Mommsen makes them say.

The first is from Cicero in the *De Republica*, II., 14.
*Numa agros quos bello Romulus ceperat divisit viritim
civibus.* The meaning of this passage is that the
lands which had been conquered by Romulus in his
wars with the neighbouring cities had not been
divided by him amongst the citizens. But it does not
prove, as we shall presently see, that the small Roman
territory occupied prior to these conquests was not
divided when the city was founded. The quotation
from Cicero applies to a certain area of land; it
does not apply to all land. It does not imply that no
division had taken place before this time ; and Cicero
does not say a single word which can refer to a period
of community.

The second reference is to Dionysius of Halicarnassus, II., 74 ; and the following is a literal translation : "Numa enacted laws concerning the boundaries
of estates ; he laid down that each man should sur-
round his land with a boundary and set up landmarks

[1] Mommsen, *Roman History*, Engl. trans., vol. i., p. 194.
This theory has been copied and reproduced word for word,
without verification, by M. Viollet and M. de Laveleye.

of stone ; he dedicated these landmarks to the god
Terminus, and ordained that sacrifices should be offered
up to him every year ; he appointed the festival of the
Terminalia." That the second king of Rome drew up
regulations for the worship of boundaries cannot be regarded as distinctly proving that before his time there
were no boundaries; and certainly it is not clear evidence that till then private property did not exist. The
historian does not say that in the preceding generation
the Romans lived under a system of common ownership
of land. On the contrary, he says a little earlier that
the founder of the city did divide the territory as other
founders were wont to do. In so doing he had paid
attention to the social divisions already existing; and
as the people were divided into thirty curiæ, he apportioned the territory into thirty lots in such a manner
that the members of each curia might remain together.
Dionysius adds that the founder, when dividing the
land, reserved a part to form the *ager publicus, i.e.,*
the property of the State. This piece of information
proves beyond doubt that in the mind of the historian
the whole territory was not *ager publicus,* as M.
Mommsen thinks. Dionysius of Halicarnassus indicates distinctly that the distinction between *ager
publicus* and *ager privatus* dates from the earliest
days of the Roman city.

The third authority quoted is Plutarch, *Life of
Numa,* 16: "The Roman city had in the beginning

only a small territory; Romulus gained for it by conquest an additional territory larger than its old one;
and the whole of this was divided by Numa amongst
the poor citizens." This passage, like the one from
Cicero, states that a division was effected by the
second king; but at the same time it draws a distinction between the two territories; and it is not
possible to draw from it the conclusion that the
district first occupied had not been already divided.

Thus not one of three passages quoted by M.
Mommsen seems to me to have the meaning he attributes to it. Not one of the three implies that the
Romans held their land in common even for a single
generation. Other authorities also, which must not
be passed over, expressly tell us of this earlier partition, the recollection of which was preserved, as was
that of everything else connected with the founding of
the city. Besides Dionysius of Halicarnassus whom
we have already referred to (II. 7), Varro, who was as
learned as a man could well be at that time, declares
that Romulus divided the territory into hereditary
portions, each consisting of but two *jugera*[1] (about an
acre and a quarter). The elder Pliny, Nonius and
Festus give us the same information.[2] But this first

[1] Varro, *De re rustica*, I. 10: "Bina jugera, quod a Romulo
primum divisa viritim, quæ heredem sequerentur."

[2] Pliny, XVIII. 2, 7: "Romulus in primis instituit. . . .
Bina tunc jugera populo Romano satis erant nullique majorem
modum attribuit." Nonius, edit. Quicherat, p. 61. Festus, v.
centuriatus ager.

partition, which is contemporaneous with the very foundation of the city, did not follow upon a period of non-division. No Roman historian makes any such statement as that the land remained for a period undivided.

M. Mommsen tries to dispose of these statements, and argues as follows : Two *jugera* are too little to support a family ; therefore we cannot consider that this was a real partition of the territory ; and it necessarily follows that the families must have lived under some kind of communistic system, with a common use of the public lands. An ingenious process of reasoning, but nothing more ; mere guess-work. The question is not as M. Mommsen thinks, whether two *jugera* are enough for the support of a family ; but rather whether the founder, who had only a very small extent of territory at his disposal, with a population already numerous, could grant more. The lots were too small, as it would appear, because the territory also was too small; but we cannot deduce from this, as M. Mommsen does, that the Romans followed some system of communism. The insufficiency of the land, besides, gives a reason for the conquests which were soon afterwards effected under Romulus.

In conclusion, it appears to me exceedingly rash to maintain that the Romans had at first a system of common ownership of land. Such a statement is not supported by any ancient authority. On the contrary, the early writers describe a partition of land which takes place at the very time when the city is founded; and the land thus divided becomes complete and hereditary property. Some years later the city conquers fresh territory; and again, with but little delay, it is divided into private property. This is all that we are told.

We are, however, able to gather that these two successive partitions were not in every respect alike. The first related only to the *ager Romanus*, i.e., to that part of the territory which was in primitive times attached to the *Urbs;* the second related to conquered territory. In the first, the ground was distributed amongst the *curiæ*, each curia then distributing it amongst its *gentes*, whence it came about that those lots for a long time retained the name of the several Roman *gentes;* in the second partition, which followed the first but did not annul it, the land was divided according to heads, *viritim.* This innovation will be seen to be of deep importance by any one who is acquainted with the ideas of the ancients and with ancient law. At the time of the first division, property still belonged to the family; at the second, it belonged to the individual. Thus, then, the two kinds of proprietary right that the ancient world successively recognised are seen, one after the other, with an interval of but forty years between. The Roman nation was one of the first to substitute individual for family property. They made use of bequest and sale from an early date. Roman law did indeed retain some traces of the early rights of the family; but what really characterises it is that it brought about the triumph of the system of individual ownership.

IV.

On the application of the comparative method to this problem.

It is impossible to deny that the comparative method is not only of use but also absolutely indispensable in dealing with a subject of this kind. In order to discover the origin of property in land among mankind it is plain that every nation must be studied; at any rate every nation that has left any trace behind it. Some part of this work of comparison had already been attempted by Maurer; but he had limited himself to the Slavonic and Scandinavian countries. A great and powerful writer, Sir Henry Maine, has applied the comparative method to India. But the first to attempt what I may call "universal comparison," is, if I mistake not, M. Emile de Laveleye, in his work, "On Property and its Primitive Forms," published in 1874. His theory is that the agricultural groups of the whole world, from India to

Scotland, for a long time cultivated the soil in common, and that " the history of all lands reveals to us a primitive condition of collectivity." M. de Laveleye is an economist; but it is by historical evidence that he endeavours to support his thesis, and it is this evidence that I shall now proceed to test. His reputation either as economist or moralist can receive no injury from a purely historical discussion.

He passes in review one after the other (I am following the order of his chapters) the Slavs of Russia, the island of Java, ancient India, the German Mark, the Arabs of Algeria, the ancient Moors of Spain, the Yoloffs of the coast of Guinea, the Afghans, the ancient Greeks, the ancient Romans, England, the Southern Slavs, Switzerland and the Netherlands. Here we have peoples of every race, every degree of latitude, and every age; yet this list does not include all nations. To mention only some of the ancient world, we do not find here the ancient Egyptians, the ancient Jews, or the ancient Assyrians, peoples which, nevertheless, are much better known than the Yoloffs, the Javanese, or the ancient Germans. Why are they not here? Can it be because all the documents concerning them, however far back we may go, bear witness to the custom of private ownership, and do not show a trace of community in land? It is certain that the history of Egypt shows the existence of property from the remotest times. It is certain that contracts for the sale of land have been discovered upon Babylonian bricks. It is certain, also, that the sacred books of the Jews refer to property and the sale of land as far back as the time of Abraham (Genesis XXIII.). Was it for this reason that they were omitted in the universal comparison of all nations? But as our author was seeking a general rule for the whole human race, and says that he has found it, he ought not to pass over a single people of whom we know anything. When one seeks to construct a general system, the facts which contradict it must be presented as well as those in its favour. This is the first rule of the comparative method.

Having insisted on this omission, of which every one will see the importance, I shall consider one by one the nations spoken of by our author, and verify his assertions.

1. Among the Slavs of Russia M. de Laveleye observes the *mir*, *i.e.*, a village dividing its soil annually or every few years among its members. In this *mir* he recognises an association with common ownership of the soil. "The *mir* alone," he says, "owns the land, and individuals have nothing more than the enjoyment of it, turn and turn about." On this I have two observations to make. In the first place, the Russian *mir* is only a village and a small village, the population rarely exceeding two hundred

souls; it always cultivates the same land; so that if
this be a communistic group it is at any rate one
which is confined to a narrow radius. The *mir* by no
means represents a "tribal community," still less a
"national community." One cannot conclude from
the *mir* that the Russian nation follows a system of
agrarian communism, or that the soil is the property
of the whole nation, or that the soil is common to
everyone; so that the example departs widely from
the thesis that is sought to be maintained.

In the second place, if we examine the *mir* as it
was before the reforms of the last Czar but one, we
discover that the *mir* is not owner of the soil, but is
itself owned by some one else. In the *mir*, lands and
men alike belong to a lord; and lord and land-owner
are one. M. de Laveleye does not deny this fact; he
even recognises "that the *mir* pays the rent to the
lord collectively." This single fact makes the whole
theory fall to the ground. Since the soil belongs not
to the *mir*, but to some one else, the *mir* does not
represent agrarian communism. It is a village, like
all our villages of the Middle Ages, which is the private
property of a single individual; the peasants are only
tenants or serfs; the only peculiarity about it is, that
these peasants who pay rent for the land collectively
also cultivate it collectively.

It is true that there are certain theorists who say:
"It is probable that there was a time when the

landlord did not exist, and when the land was possessed in common by the peasants." This is precisely what would have to be proved. They ought first to prove that the landowner or lord at one time did not exist, and next that the peasants then possessed the land in common. Now these are two propositions in support of which no one has ever been able to bring forward proof or even an appearance of proof. On the contrary, according to M. Tchitchérin and other writers who have studied the subject, it has been proved that the association of the *mir* has only been in existence for three hundred years; that it was created in the year 1592; and that far from being the result of a spontaneous and ancient growth, it was instituted by the act of a despotic Government, by an ukase of the Czar Fédor Ivanovitch. Before this epoch land in Russia was an object of private property; so one is led to believe by the documents of donation and bequest quoted by M. Tchitchérin. I am aware that the question is still warmly discussed and remains obscure; but so long as documents proving the existence of the *mir* before the 16th century are not produced, we must continue to doubt whether the *mir* is an ancient institution at all. So far as we know at present, it only came into existence with the feudal period; it forms one of the wheels of the feudal organisation in Russia—a group of serfs, which the Government requires to cultivate its land in common, so as to be more

sure of the payment of the rent. Far from being
collective ownership, the *mir* is collective serfdom.
That, at any rate, is what appears from the material in
our possession. Theorists are at perfect liberty to
hope that new documents will come to light which
will show the contrary. Till then, it is impossible to
bring forward the *mir* as a proof that the human race
once practised agrarian communism.

2. M. de Laveleye passes on to the island of Java,
and describes the condition of things there in a
chapter full of interest; in some places the soil
is cultivated in common, it is in others annually divided. But I cannot help noticing that
throughout he is speaking of the present time.
He describes the condition of things as they are
now. He makes use of the regulations of the Dutch
Government, of laws of 1853, of parliamentary
reports of 1869. The furthest date to which he goes
back is to certain regulations of 1806. And yet,
since he is dealing with the problem of the origin of
property, what one wants to hear about is the
ancient state of things. I am aware that some people
will at once say "such a system must be old;"
but a student who has any critical instinct will
rather say that the present existence of such a
system proves nothing at all in relation to earlier
times. And, indeed, we read in one of the reports on
which M. de Laveleye relies, that " this system began

with the cultivation of indigo, sugar and coffee for the benefit of the Dutch Government."[1] The sort of communism we are now considering would in this case be but a recent institution, a creation of the European conquerors. It is true that others make it commence earlier, with the cultivation of rice.[2] This is easily explained : " Rice growing in water requires a system of irrigation, which would be impossible without association ; and this necessity gives rise to the practice of common cultivation." It has been ascertained how these villages arose. " Several families agree to establish a system of irrigation in common. As the water has been brought by the co-operation of all, the result is that the land irrigated by it is cultivated by all."[3] But it is apparent that the soil does not belong to the nation or the tribe ; it belongs to a group, an association. An association of proprietors is not communism ; it is one of the forms of property.

We must also observe that private property does exist in Java. In six out of the twenty provinces of the island that alone is to be found, and association is unknown; in eight the two methods are practised side by side; in six association is only practised on the rice fields and irrigated lands, and the rest of the land is

---

[1] M. de Laveleye, *De la propriété collective du sol*, in the *Revue de Belgique*, 1886, p. 50 of the reprint.

[2] *Ibidem*, p. 49.

[3] *Ibidem*, p. 65.

held entirely as private property. From these facts I cannot draw the conclusion that community in land was a primitive and natural institution in the island of Java. We meet with it only under modern circumstances, and even here we must recognise that it is less a community than an association.

8. Our author next devotes a few words to ancient India, and here I shall imitate his brevity. He gives but one reference; a sentence from Nearchus, the officer of Alexander the Great. I shall give it first as translated by M. de Laveleye, and then as it really is. "Nearchus informs us that in certain districts of India the land was cultivated in common *by tribes*, which, at the close of the year, divided the crop among them.' Now the Greek signifies: "In other parts the work of agriculture is carried on *by each family* in common, κατὰ συγγένειαν κοινῇ; and when the crops have been gathered each person takes his share for his support during the year."[1] We see that M. de Laveleye had overlooked the words κατὰ συγγένειαν. He has mistaken a community of the family for a community of the tribe. I know that many people only too readily identify the two things; but a little

[1] Strabo, xv., 1., 66, edit. Didot, p. 610: παρ' ἄλλοις δὲ κατὰ συγγένειαν κοινῇ τοὺς καρποὺς ἐργασαμένων, ἐπὰν συγκομίσωσιν, αἱρεῖσθαι ἕκαστον εἰς διατροφὴν τοῦ ἔτους. If one reads the whole chapter, one sees that Nearchus, who distinguishes between general and exceptional institutions, τὰ μὲν κοινά, τὰ δὲ ἴδια, includes this among the exceptional.

attention will show that they are essentially different. When a family, even though it may form a large group of persons, cultivates its land in common, this is not agrarian communism; it is merely an undivided family and undivided family property.

4. M. de Laveleye next speaks of the Germanic mark. Here he does not do more than reproduce Maurer's theory, on which he relies without apparently having verified a single one of his references.

5. Then follows a chapter on agrarian communities amongst the Arabs of Algeria, the Moors of Spain, the Yoloffs of the coast of Guinea, the Mexicans, the Caribeans, the Afghans and the Tchérémisses. A story or sentence from some traveller is quoted about each of these nations. As to this I have one remark to make: there is nothing rarer or more difficult than an accurate observation. This truth, which is recognised in all other sciences, ought also to be recognised by every one who is dealing with history; for history is precisely that one of all the sciences in which observation is most difficult and demands the greatest attention. A traveller makes the general statement that amongst the Caribeans or the Yoloffs he has seen a partition of land, or has been told that such a thing was customary. But has he observed between whom the partition took place ? Was it amongst the members of the same family, or amongst all the inhabitants of the same village, or between the villages and all the

various parts of the tribe or nation? These are
shades of differences that a hasty traveller cannot
notice, and that an historian equally hasty refrains
from inquiring into. And yet, the character and consequences of the partition depend altogether upon the
answer to this question. The study of a social system
is a serious undertaking, and one not often to be met
with in travellers' tales.

And then we must ask whether, side by side with
certain facts reported by travellers, there are not others
which contradict them. You see common land among
certain Arab tribes; but it must also be noticed that
the Koran recognises private property, and that it has
existed among the Arabs from time immemorial.[1]
There are other nations where you may meet with examples of land held in common, but where, nevertheless, it must be acknowledged that private property
greatly preponderates. In Spain, for instance, we are
told that "in certain villages the land is divided anew
each year amongst the inhabitants."[2] In how many
villages? Two ardent inquirers, whose only desire
was to find proofs of this community in land, M. Oliveira
Martins and M. de Azcarate, found it in only four
villages in the whole Iberian peninsula.[3] Perhaps

---

[1] See the work of M. Eug. Robe, *Origines de la propriété
immobilière en Algérie*, 1883—a volume which is full of facts.

[2] Em. de Laveleye, *De la propriété*, p. 105.

[3] *Id.*, *La propriété collective*, in the *Revue de Belgique*, 1886
pp. 2-24 of the reprint.

you will think that these are vestiges of an earlier
state of things that may once have been general.
Not at all. It has been proved that in these four
villages the system of common ownership did not appear until the twelfth or thirteenth century, A.D.; and
the particular causes which led to its appearance are
well known. This kind of community was, therefore,
neither general nor ancient. M. de Laveleye also
mentions a village community in Italy; but it is one
which was only created in 1263. A certain estate of
about 5000 acres had till that date belonged to a private
owner; that is, it had been precisely the opposite of
common property. In 1263 the owner, who happened
to be a bishop, gave it to the tenants, on condition
that they held it in common. Can a few isolated
facts like this prove that mankind used to hold land
in common in primitive times?

6. M. de Laveleye's theory would be incomplete and
insecure if he did not manage to bring in the Greeks
and Romans. He does little more than repeat the
authorities used by M. de Viollet. Like him, he believes that the legend of a golden age—of an age, that
is, when man did not till the soil (for this is the
distinctive and essential point in all these legends),—is
a proof that nations held land in common at a period
when they did till the soil; he even adds that " he is
forced to arrive at the conclusion that the ancient
poets depicted in the golden age a state of civilisation

(sic) of which the recollection had been handed down to later times."[1] Like M. Viollet, he quotes the passages from Virgil, Tibullus and Trogus Pompeius without looking to see whether these passages describe a condition of civilisation or one of barbarism. He tells us what Porphyrus says about the 2000 disciples gathered together by Pythagoras in his phalanstery. He quotes the sentence from Diodorus about the Lipari isles; without seeing that it distinctly describes the institution of private property. Trusting in M. Viollet, ho borrows his pages on the *cryzis* and the Spartan *συσσίτια*; for, like him, he believes that these common meals, from which Aristotle tells us that the poorer Spartans were excluded, were "a communistic institution."[2]

M. de Laveleye also believes that the division of land at the founding of each city implies an earlier stage in which the city cultivated the land in common. He does not notice that this division, taking place at the very moment when the city is founded, is not the result of an earlier state of communism. It is the earliest fact to which we can go back. So soon as a band of emigrants have made themselves masters of a territory, they parcel it out in lots with complete and hereditary ownership. With very rare exceptions, a Greek city did not hold or cultivate land in common for a single year.

[1] Em. de Laveleye, *De la propriété*, p. 162.   [2] *Ibidem*, p. 161.

These lots were called κλῆροι in Greek, *sortes* in Latin, because they were originally drawn by lot. M. de Laveleye, noticing these two words, at once concludes that the drawing by lot took place every year (p. 85). This is a mistake. Out of all the cases where you find mention of a partition, you will not find one in which it was annual or periodical. In every case the division referred to takes place once and for all, in perpetuity.[1] Each portion is henceforward hereditary in the family to which it has fallen by lot; and this is the reason why κλῆρος had the meaning of inheritance and *sors* signified patrimony.

The prohibition against selling the land, *i.e.*, against separating it from the family in order to transfer it to another family or even to bestow it on the State, appears to M. de Laveleye a proof that the land belonged to the State (p. 166). It is merely a proof that according to the ideas of the ancients it ought always to belong to the same family. M. de Laveleye reproaches me with having, in the *Cité Antique*, attributed this prohibition of sale " to the influence of ancient religion." The phrase gives an incorrect idea of my meaning. What I showed was that family property was closely bound up with family religion. Sale outside the family was not permitted because

---

[1] Save in the exceptional case described by Diodorus in the Lipari islands.

ancient law and ancient belief connected the land with the family. The land belonged to the family, not to the individual. It was the same, in my opinion amongst the ancient Germans and the Slavs; and hence it was that amongst all these nations ancient law did not permit the sale of land.

For the same reason bequest was prohibited among the Greeks, Italians, Germans, and Slavs in the early period of their law. The land must pass to the son or the nearest relations. For the same reason, again, the daughter did not inherit; because by her marriage she would have carried the land out of the family. All these facts, which it is now impossible not to admit, are unmistakable signs of a condition in which property belonged to the family. They are all directly contrary to a condition of communism.

M. de Laveleye also lays great stress upon Sparta; only he omits to mention that private property was established there from the first beginning of the city, and that every κλῆρος remained attached to the same family down to the revolution of Cleomenes, i.e., for eight centuries.[1] To make up for that, he tells us of certain imaginary brotherhoods, "which must have played an important part in the social body;" a

[1] This is shown by Heraclides of Pontus in the *Fragmenta hist. graec.*, of Didot, vol. II., p. 211; and by Plutarch, *Life of Agis*, 5. To this can be added the other texts cited in my *I trade sur la propriété à Sparte*, 1880. See also the work of M. Claudio Jannet.

statement for which there is no authority. He adds
that Sparta "had a wide extent of common land;"
for which also there is no evidence: and that "this
common land was used to provide for the public
meals;" which is directly opposed to the definite
evidence we do possess.

He accumulates quotations, but they are inexact.
He refers to Aristotle (*Polit.* vii., 10); but all Aristotle
says is that men began by being hunters and shep-
herds; does that imply that when they became
agriculturists they held the soil in common? He
quotes Virgil, who in the Æneid (xi. 315) says that
"the Aurunci tilled the land in common;" turn to
the passage; the expression "in common" is not
there; M. de Laveleye has unconsciously added it
himself. Every writer does this who is under
the influence of a fixed idea.[1] Speaking of Rome,
he declares "that he sees a proof of primitive
community in the common meals of the *curiæ;*" and
he does not notice that these repasts of the *curia*
only took place on certain festivals, and that they
were sacred feasts, as we are expressly told by

[1] In the same way he cites Ælian, V. 9, as saying that the
inhabitants of Locri and Rhegium cultivated the land in common.
What Ælian says is that " the cities of Locri and Rhegium have
made a treaty which permits the inhabitants of the one town to
settle on the territory of the other." Of common cultivation
there is not a word. These authorities are given in the article
by M. de Laveleye, in *Revue de Belgique,* 1886, pp. 9 *et seq.* of
the reprint.

Dionysius of Halicarnassus, who witnessed them. "The *curiæ*," he says, "with their priests, perform sacrifices and eat together on feast days." This is not an agrarian community; it is a religious communion. Suppose that a stranger, seeing a number of good Christians communicating in our churches, declared that he saw in this a proof that the French held their land in common! A little farther we read: "The law of the Twelve Tables preserves a trace of common ownership; for in default of the *proximus agnatus* the *gens* is preferred to the other *agnates*." There is nothing resembling this in what we have of the law of the Twelve Tables; the gens was never preferred to the agnates. Our author quotes, it is true, the following sentence, which he attributes to Gaius: *in legitimis hereditatibus successio non est: gentiles familiam habento*, which is said to be in Gaius iii., 12; but look in Gaius for this extraordinary sentence, and you certainly will not find it. Thus, alike for Greece and for Rome, M. de Laveleye has got together a number of authorities; but there is not a single quotation that is exact, or that has the meaning he attributes to it.

7. We now come to the Southern Slavs, *i.e.*, the Bosnians, Servians, and Bulgarians, who, in their turn, have to furnish arguments in support of the theory.[1] This chapter of M. de Laveleye's is the most

---

[1] *De la propriété et de ses formes primitives*, p. 201.

interesting in the book, the most curious, and, in my
opinion, the most exact. Only I do not see how it
bears upon the problem with which we are occupied.
It is very true that the Servian or Bosnian village
often cultivates its land in common. But this village
is composed of a small group of from twenty to sixty
persons, who dwell in four or five houses built within
a single enclosure; and the land belonging to it seldom
exceeds sixty acres. Look at it closely, and you will
see that this little village is nothing more than a
family. M. de Laveleye recognises this (p. 204). The
brothers as a rule keeping together and the family
continuing to form one undivided body, the property
remains united like the family. The land is cultivated
in common and the produce is consumed in common,
under the direction of the head of the family. This
is described by M. de Laveleye with zest and ability;
but it is not community in land; it is the common
ownership of the family. We have seen it amongst
the ancient Greeks; in the most ancient Roman law;
amongst the Germans; and now we find it amongst the
Servians. The family forms a small village; it keeps
to itself on its own land; and this land is a common
possession which has belonged to it from time immemorial. It must be added that all the characteristics which accompany family ownership amongst
the Greeks and Germans are to be found here. The
custom of bequest does not exist, nor does that of gift

or sale. All the members of a family are common owners of the soil, and consequently they alone are the heirs. Anyone leaving the family loses his rights over the land; anyone entering it by adoption has the same rights as those who were born into it. Except that the chief is no longer the eldest member or the son of the eldest, but the one whom the rest elect—a change which naturally came about in the course of time—this family resembles in every other respect the ancient Greek family. But that the soil belongs to the nation or the tribe there is not the slightest evidence.

8. M. de Laveleye now comes to the *allmenden* of Switzerland. He tells us "that never was there a more radical democracy than that which was to be found in primitive Switzerland," and he describes the *Landgemeinde,* "which goes back to the earliest times" (pages 270 *et seq*). "The *Allmend,*" he says again, "presents the ancient type of true justice, which ought to serve as the basis for the society of the future" (p. 282).

I should like to learn, however, whether these *allmenden* really do come down from remote times. Our author tells us so, but without bringing forward any kind of proof. He declares "that they go back to the patriarchal period" (p. 291), "that they have lasted for thousands of years" (p. 281). It is easy to say this; but on what evidence does it rest ? Private property exists in Switzerland, and our author cannot point to any epoch in which it did not exist. If we examine the law of the Burgundians and of the Alamanni, by which the country was first governed, it is private property we find, not common ownership. If we examine the charters down to the 12th century, we still find private property. The *allmenden* of to-day certainly date back some six or seven centuries. Can they be traced farther back than that?

And what exactly are these *allmenden*? Do we see in them a system of non-division of land, a system, that is, under which the land, being considered the common property of the whole people, is not supposed to belong to anyone individually? By no means. Private property is in full force in Switzerland, side by side with the *allmenden*. The *allmenden* are only a part of the land of each village and indeed the smallest part, a tenth, or, at most, a fifth. They are usually forests, mountain pastures, or marshes, and include very little land capable of cultivation. Private property is accordingly the dominant fact; common ownership only concerns accessories.

The *allmenden* are just what is to be found in every country; they are the village commons. It would be interesting and instructive if we could discover their origin, just as it is interesting to inquire into the origin of the commons in France. But village commons do not in any way prove a general system of common ownership; and no one has yet been able to prove that they are the outcome of such a system. We know that when the Romans founded a colony, they instituted private property from the very first; but at the same time they reserved a portion of the soil, which was to be the common possession of the new city. And to go farther back, we know that Rome herself, from the time she first appears in history, had an *ager publicus* at the same time as *agri privati*, and that the Greek cities also had a γῆ δημοσία. This public land was in no way an indication that the people lived a single day without individual estates. The *allmenden* of Switzerland are commons of the same character as we find everywhere else. Each village has its own; and they are the property of the village, which sometimes sells them, lets them to the highest bidder, or sells the wood upon them, to defray the expenses of its school or church. Frequently the commons are left for the inhabitants to use as they like; and they get wood from them, graze their cattle there, or cultivate small portions. But it is important to notice that only those who own land in the village have any rights of enjoyment over the *allmend*. I refer chiefly to the condition of things before the last forty years: for only quite recently have such rights been extended to mere residents and the inhabitants generally. In essential characteristics the *allmend* is not common property; it does not belong to all; it is held in common by people who are already owners of land. It is an appendage of private property.

M. de Laveleye has written some beautiful passages on the usefulness of these commons, on the mistake which has been made in France in their general alienation, and on the happy results produced by them in Switzerland, both in almost entirely preventing the growth of absolute destitution and in attaching the poorest peasant to his native soil. These considerations are just, profound, and inspired by generous feeling, although but little applicable to modern society. But we are now considering them in relation to the supposed common ownership of land; with that the *allmenden* have nothing to do, and they prove nothing as to its earlier existence.

9. M. de Laveleye finally refers to the Scotch townships as a proof of primitive community.[1] In the more distant parts of Scotland, especially in certain islands lying to the north-west, we find groups of people who hold the land of a village in common and divide it amongst themselves in separate lots every year. Is this a system of land communism, or, as it is called, collective ownership ? At the first glance one would think so. But if you are not satisfied with a first glance and look further, you will observe that the

---

[1] *La propriété collective du sol*, in the *Revue de Belgique*, 1886. He repeats the argument in the *Revue socialiste*, 1888, p. 452, and in the *Revue d'économie politique*, July, 1888.

village belongs to a single person, the landlord. The peasants are nothing more than the cultivators. M. de Laveleye cannot help recognising this : " The land of the village," he says, " is let to them by the owner." Again : " The land does not belong to them ; it is the property of a landlord to whom they pay rent for it." The cultivators act together as an association " with the consent of the landlord ; " and there are villages in which the landlord does not allow this collective system of occupation. " They have a head who is generally appointed by the landlord." The rent is paid collectively. We have a description of the *township* in a work published recently. The house of the lord, the *domus dominica* of our charters, stands in the centre of the village, by the side of the church.[1] It is built of stone ; and around it, at a little distance, stand the dwellings of the "villeins," built of mud and thatched with straw. The villeins owe their lord rent and certain personal services.

We see from this that the Scotch or English township is not a community which owns its own land ; it is the property of an individual owner, and the only thing about it which is collective is the cultivation. The township is really a private estate ; and the group of peasants who till it in common are the tenants. Ownership and tenancy are two distinct things, which

---

[1] Isaac Taylor, in the *Contemporary Review*, Dec., 1886, referred to by M. de Laveleye.

must not be confused. To be owners in common is very different from being tenants in common under a landlord. We find in France also, throughout the Middle Ages, instances of tenancies in common; and I know that there are writers who are quick to identify them with ownership in common.[1] But this is a mistake which no one can make who has any accuracy of thought; for it is quite evident that whilst the land was cultivated by a common group of peasants, it belonged to a lord who stood above them. The Scotch township has no connection whatever with an ancient system of community in land.

M. de Laveleye puts forward an hypothesis; he supposes that there was an earlier period in which the township belonged to the peasants themselves, and the lord, whom we find in later times, did not exist. But this is a mere hypothesis unsupported by a single document or a single fact. He goes further and maintains that this system of village communities was in force throughout the whole of England in the Saxon period. But there is no evidence for this in the Anglo-Saxon laws; they give not the slightest indication of it. The *tuncipesmot* is not community in land; nor is the *folcland*. We must never lose sight of the fact that history is based upon documents, and not upon hypotheses or flights of the imagination. When M.

---

[1] *E.g.*, M. P. Viollet in all the latter part of the article already referred to.

de Laveleye says that "the English manor has de-
stroyed the old village community," he makes an
entirely hypothetical generalisation. To imagine the
manorial lord of the Middle Ages as a warrior who has
forcibly set himself over a community of free men, is
to show that one knows nothing of the documents from
the fifth to the tenth centuries, and that one has an
altogether childish idea of the origin of feudalism.

To come back to the comparative method. I believe
that it is infinitely fruitful; but only on condition that
the facts which are compared have a real resemblance
to one another, and that things which are widely different are not confused. When you bring together the
Scotch township which is nothing more than an
association of tenants, the Russian *mir* which seems
to have long been only an association of serfs, the
Servian village which, on the other hand, is a house-
hold community, and the *allmend* or commons which
are a consequence and accompaniment of private property, you confuse things which are absolutely different, and which, moreover, are very far removed from
the system of community in land that you are anxious
to prove.

It is needful to come to an understanding as to
what the "comparative method" really is. I have
observed that, during the last fifteen years or so,
there has been a strange misapprehension on this
point. Some writers maintain that to compare any

I

facts, no matter what, is to apply the comparative method. They search all over the world for peculiar usages; they cite the legend of the golden age amongst the ancients as if it were an historical fact; they seize upon a trifling circumstance which occurred in the Lipari Isles as if it related to the entire Greek world; they seize upon some custom, such as public repasts or the festivals of the curia; thence they pass to the Russian *mir* and talk of it as if they knew all about it; then they describe a township or an *allmend*; and, in short, whenever they find an instance of anything that is done in common, at once they suppose that they have discovered community in land. They pretend they have discovered the most wide-spread institutions of the human race by the help of some few instances that they have sought for far and wide, and that they do not take the trouble to observe accurately. And, what is a more serious matter, they omit and leave out of their consideration facts which are constant, normal, well-authenticated, which are engraven in the laws of all peoples, and which have made up their historical life. They give us a few isolated facts and turn our thoughts away from permanent institutions. This is not the comparative method.

If you wished to employ the comparative method it would first of all be needful to study each nation in itself, to study it throughout its history, and above all

in its law. Should you wish to know if the ancient
Greek cities held their land in common, you must
study Greek law. For the Romans, you must go over
the whole history of Rome; for the Germans, you
must take German law. M. Viollet and M. de Laveleye
make frequent references to ancient India; why do
they not mention that in all the ancient Hindoo law
that has come down to us the rights of private property are sanctioned, although, of course, the holding
of property in common by co-heirs is also recognised ?
Why has no one quoted the old maxim: "The land
belongs to the man who first clears it, as the deer belongs to the man who first wounds it" ? They prefer
to quote certain customs, whose importance they enormously exaggerate, rather than present to us the rules
which were constant and normal. The comparative
method does not consist in discovering amongst fifteen
different nations fifteen little facts, which, if interpreted in a certain manner, unite in the construction
of a system; it consists in studying a number of
nations in regard to their law, their ideas, all the
circumstances of their social life, and in discovering
what they have in common and wherein they differ.
I greatly fear that this comparative method, when it
shall be seriously applied, will give very different
results than those that MM. Viollet and de Laveleye
believe they have obtained from the comparative
method as they understand it.

V.

On community of land amongst the Gauls.

It would be indeed surprising had the supporters of this theory not applied it to the ancient Gauls. So little is known about them, that it is very tempting and not very difficult to introduce community in land into their history.

One single fact, however, ought to stand in the way; it is that Cæsar, whose book is the only authority which has historical value, nowhere tells us that land was common amongst the Gauls. His silence on this point is not a thing which can be passed over. It is, indeed, in the eyes of every one accustomed to historical research, a very significant fact. It is true that Cæsar does not expressly state that private property was the custom amongst the Gauls. For a writer who is only speaking in passing of Gallic institutions, to omit to call attention to a law of property which was in conformity with what he was accustomed to, is not the same thing as to omit to mention a communism which would be the opposite of what he was accustomed to, and which would strike him by its very strangeness. It must be noticed that Cæsar is not describing the entire social condition of

the Gauls; he contents himself with mentioning
those customs which have struck him as being
very different from those he saw in Italy. We have
only to read the ten paragraphs which he devotes to
this subject, to recognise this. After describing in
three paragraphs what was peculiar in their political
organisation, and in three more what was peculiar in
their religion, he passes on to what was peculiar in
their private life, and he begins as follows—"As to
the institutions of private life, the following are those
wherein they differ from other nations." By "other
nations" Cæsar clearly means the nations that he knew
that is, primarily, the Italians and Greeks. This open-
ing sentence makes it plain that Cæsar intended only
to tell us of characteristics which were peculiar to
the Gauls. He is going to mention differences, not
resemblances. If private property is the custom there
as it is in Rome, it will not be necessary to say so; but
if it is not the custom, he will say so. His absolute silence
on this point is a proof that the Gauls did not sensibly
differ from the Italians in the matter; his silence implies that they were not ignorant of private property.
We must remember that the entire absence of private
property would have appeared so strange to a Roman
that it could not have escaped Cæsar's notice. He
observed it in Germany where he passed only eighteen
days; he would certainly have discovered it in Gaul
where he passed eight summers. If he does not

mention community in land, it is obviously because it did not exist.

But we have evidence even more convincing. Going on to speak of the Germans, he remarks that he will explain "in what they differ from the Gauls, *quo differant hae nationes inter sese*" (vi., 11); and further on: "The Germans differ much from this manner of life of the Gauls, *Germani multum ab hac consuetudine differunt.*" He then draws the following contrast between the two nations: 1, the Germans have no Druids; 2, the Germans have not the same gods as the Gauls; 3, and lastly, the Germans have not private property. Is not this remark as to the difference between the two nations almost the same thing as if Cæsar had said that the Gauls recognised private property and held their land in individual ownership?

This is not all. Cæsar uses an expression in which he indirectly and almost unconsciously bears witness to the existence of property in land amongst the Gauls. In Book VI., Chapter 13, he says that the Druids act as judges in almost all suits, criminal as well as civil.[1]

[1] "Fere de omnibus controversiis publicis privatisque constituunt." It is well known that in legal language, the *judicia publica* are criminal cases; as the term implies, cases which concern crimes punished by a public authority; the *judicia privata* are those which concern private interests alone, and in which the State is not involved. See on this distinction Paul, *Sententiae*, I., 5, 2; Ulpian XIII., 2; *Fragmenta Vaticana*, 197 and 326; *Digest*, XLVII., tit. 1 and 2; XLVIII., I.; I., 1, 1,

He then gives a list of the disputes brought before
them, and amongst criminal offences he instances
murder; amongst civil suits he mentions " those concerning inheritance or boundaries," *ei de hereditate, ei
de finibus controversia est.* If there were in Gaul suits
concerning inheritance or boundaries, it must have
meant that the Gauls had a system of inheritance and
made use of boundaries; *i.e.*, that land was private and
hereditary property. Cæsar says elsewhere that the
Germans have no *fines*; he says here that the Gauls
have them.

We cannot say whether the institution of private
property in Gaul was exactly similar to that of private
property in Rome; whether it had the same legal
guarantees; whether its boundaries had the same in-
violable character. We do not even know if property
still belonged to the family or was already in the
hands of individual owners. Cæsar only tells us one
thing, and that is, that it existed; for "inheritance
and boundaries" are unmistakable signs of private
ownership, and as clearly disprove a system of
corporate land-holding.[1]

§ 6; XXIII., 2, 43, § 11 and 12. To translate *controversia publica*
in the passage from Cæsar as disputes between two peoples
would run counter to the meaning of words. *Publicus* never
means *inter duos populos.*

[1] It may be added that the social condition described by
Cæsar is irreconcilable with agrarian communism, vi., 13: *In
omni Gallia plebs paene servorum habetur loco*, etc. Notice the

This is the conclusion to which we are brought by
a simple and unbiased perusal of Cæsar's account. But
preconceptions have great force; and if a writer starts
with the idea that community in land was once
universal, the result will be that, in the face of all
evidence, and yet in perfect good faith, he will think
he finds it amongst the Gauls. One of the first
scholars of the day, M. d'Arbois de Jubainville,
whose works on the Middle Ages and on Irish literature have been so highly appreciated, thinks that the
Gauls of the time of Cæsar were not far enough
advanced in civilisation to hold private property; and
setting out with this idea, the offspring of imagination, he supposes that he can see evidence of undivided tenure. The fact that Cæsar never mentions
this troubles him very little. That Cæsar does mention, as a point of difference between the Germans
and Gauls, that the former do not hold private property, he omits to notice. And lastly, when Cæsar
refers in so many words to inheritance and boundaries
amongst the Gauls, he disposes of this somewhat
embarrassing statement by interpreting it in a most
unexpected fashion.

numerous clients of Orgetorix, i., 4; those of Vercingetorix,
vii., 4; the many poor, not in the towns, but in the country,
in agris agentes, vii., 4; the burden of the *tributa*, vi., 13.
These traits are not those of a society where the land is common.
They point rather to a system of great estates, with the soil in
the hands of the magnates.

In his opinion, when Cæsar mentions suits concerning inheritance, *de hereditate*, it is impossible that the inheritances of private persons should be in question, as the custom of inheritance did not exist. Then what was the inheritance referred to by Cæsar? According to M. de Jubainville, he was speaking of succession to the crown. Sovereignty existed; the sons of kings wished to succeed their fathers; and if a dispute arose, the Druids acted as judges. M. de Jubainville has omitted to notice that Cæsar gives at least ten instances of sons who wished to be kings like their fathers; and that in not one of these instances was the dispute carried before the Druids. It is a grave error to suppose that the Druids were accustomed to meddle in affairs of State; we have not a single example of their doing so. And yet M. de Jubainville maintains that in Cæsar *de hereditate* means the succession to the throne; and for this he gives the following reason,—that in another book, speaking of the Egyptians, Cæsar uses the expression *hereditas regni*.[1] The argument is a strange one. I reply that if Cæsar elsewhere wrote *hereditas regni*, it was because the word *hereditas* could not, when used alone, bear the meaning of the inheritance of sovereignty. It is quite certain that if Cæsar had meant to say that the Gauls brought before

[1] This appears in the *Comptes rendus de l'Académie des inscriptions et belles-lettres*, 1867, pp. 68, et seq.

the Druids their disputes as to succession to the crown, he would have said *de hereditate regnum.*

With regard to the expression, *de finibus*, M. de Jubainville will have it mean "frontiers between nations." In this he is doubly wrong, both historically and philologically. To begin with the historical error, Cæsar tells us of numerous quarrels amongst Gallic tribes; and these quarrels are never carried before the Druids. Are we to think that Cæsar said that the Druids settled disputes about frontiers, when he knew perfectly well that Druids did not decide them? It is absolutely incorrect to say that the Druids had the right of judging between tribes.[1] Moreover, when Cæsar enumerates the principal matters which had to be tried, he mentions murder as well as inheritance and boundaries; and it is impossible to doubt that he is thinking of the murder of a single person, the inheritance of a single owner, the boundaries of a single estate.

Philologically, M. de Jubainville maintains that the word *fines* may be used for the boundaries of a nation

---

[1] M. de Jubainville has translated *controrersiæ publicæ*, as if it were *controrersiæ inter duos populos*. I know of no example in Latin literature where the word *publicus* has this sense. In Suetonius, *Augustus*, 29, the *judicia publica* are certainly not suits between peoples: they are criminal suits. When Cicero, defending Roscius of Ameria, says he is conducting his first *causa publica*, it is clear that he is not arguing for one people against another. He is defending Roscius, who is accused of parricide: it is a criminal proceeding.

as well as for those of an estate. No doubt. The
word is even used in a philosophical sense, and Cicero
wrote a treatise, *De finibus bonorum et malorum.*
In every language there are words of wide application; but the student is not misled by this. In
philosophy he understands *fines* in a philosophical
sense. If a general at the head of an army is crossing
the territory of several nations, he understands *fines*
in the sense of frontiers. If it is a question of private
law, he will not doubt that *fines* is connected with
individual rights; that it means the boundaries of an
estate or a field. Now the passage in which Cæsar
speaks of "suits concerning inheritance and boundaries" is one which deals entirely with law and justice.

M. de Jubainville has taken the trouble to count
the number of times that *fines* occurs in the *De Bello
Gallico* as applied to national or tribal frontiers, and
finds they are seventy-seven. This is one of those
arguments based on statistics which impress most
people by an appearance of matter-of-fact appro-
priateness. But look at it more closely. Is the *De
Bello Gallico* a book of private law? It is a history
of military campaigns, and of negotiations between
nations; and it is very natural that the author should
frequently speak of the frontiers or the territory of
these nations. If he had written a work on law, of
which he was quite capable, he would have spoken
throughout of the boundaries of private estates.

Ought one to be surprised at this? Read Thiers' thirty volumes; make the same calculation that M. de Jubainville did for the *De Bello Gallico;* and, if you follow the same method of reasoning, you will come to the conclusion that the French are unacquainted with boundaries to private property.

What is more important to remark is, that in the whole work, in the midst of the history of wars, there occur only seven paragraphs on the customs of the Gauls and their institutions in times of peace (VI., 11, 13, 15, 18, 19, 21, 22).   Now, in these seven chapters you will find the word *fines* used three times in the unmistakable sense of boundaries of fields.[1] And so we see that, when Cæsar is speaking of wars, he uses *fines* in the sense of the frontiers of a country, and, when he is speaking of law, he uses it in the sense of the boundaries of private property. And, if we are partial to figures, we may notice that while M. de Jubainville has counted up seventy-seven *fines* in ·three hundred and forty chapters, I have counted three in seven chapters. The proportion is well kept.

But instead of making this calculation it would have been better to have noticed something which is of far more importance; in every instance where the word signifies a frontier, its meaning is unmistakably indicated by the addition of the name of

---

[1] Cæsar, vi. 22 : *Nec quisquam (apud Germanos)* FINES habet *proprios.   Ibidem : ne latos* FINES *parare studeant, potentior-esque humiliores possessionibus expellant.*

the people in question. Thus Cæsar says, *fines Hel-vetiorum*, *fines Sequanorum*, *fines Santonum*, *fines Ædurorum*, *fines Lingonum*, *fines Ambianorum*, and so on without exception.[1] Take the seventy-seven examples collected by M. de Jubainville, and you will see that the word *fines*, when it means frontiers, is always followed by the word "people," or by the name of a people. If Cæsar had wished to speak of trials about national boundaries, he would have said *controversiæ de finibus populorum*. If he did not so express himself, it was because he was speaking of boundaries in the most restricted sense of the word.

M. de Jubainville might have found this very same phrase, which he has twisted so strangely, *si de finibus controversia est*, in Cicero. We have it there word for word; *si de finibus controversia est* in Chapter X. of the *Topics*. Let us see whether in this case it can apply to the frontiers of a people. Cicero, giving an example of a definition, writes: " When you say *si de finibus controversia est*, the boundaries of private estates are clearly meant.'[2]

[1] Or else the same thing is implied by the turn of the sentence, i. 5 : *Helvetii a finibus suis exeunt* ; iv. 3 : *quem Suevi Ubios finibus expellere non possunt* ; vi. 23 : *circum fines rejiciunt civitatis* ; v. 16 : *fines regni sui* ; v. 27 : *Ambiorix tribus iter per fines suos publicet*. By a natural transition, *fines* comes to mean sometimes, not only the boundaries, but also the territory itself, vi. 42 : *ut Ambiorigis fines depopularentur*.

[2] Cicero, *Topics*, 10 : *Si de finibus controversia est, fines agrorum esse videntur*.

And so the passage from Cæsar cannot be explained away as M. de Jubainville would wish. He cannot get rid of the fact that Cæsar records in so many words that inheritance and boundaries were to be found amongst the Gauls; the very opposite, that is, of community in land. He gets together from other sources a variety of arguments which appear to him to show that the Gauls held their land in common. They are as follows: 1, Polybius says (II. 17) that the Gauls of Italy did not cultivate the land; 2, in Cæsar's time the Helvetii wished to leave their country in order to settle in a more fruitful one; 3, the Ædui admitted into their country ten thousand Boii and gave them land; 4, there was in Gallic law a custom according to which a husband and wife threw into a common stock an equal portion of the possessions of each, and allowed the income arising from this property to accumulate, so that the whole, principal and interest, might belong to the survivor. These four circumstances are supposed to prove that private property in land did not exist.[1]

Not one of the four appears to me to bear with it this consequence. Examine them one by one. I. The passage from Polybius refers, not to the Gauls of his own time, but to the Gauls who invaded Italy five centuries before, and who drove out the Etruscans

[1] D'Arbois de Jubainville, in the *Comptes rendus de l'Académie des inscriptions*, 1887, reprint, pp. 4-22.

from the district of the Po. The historian says that these invaders, being inclined to pursue their conquests, did not at first settle down and cultivate the soil, but lived on the produce of their herds. His information bears upon the Gauls at one particular moment in their history, at the time when they were planning an attack upon central Italy. It proves nothing at all about the Gauls in general, and certainly nothing about the Gauls of the time of Cæsar.

II. That the Helvetii wished to emigrate does not imply that they lived under a system of community in land. It merely implies that they preferred the soft climate and fertile plains of the south-west of Gaul to their own rugged and mountainous country. Is it an unknown thing for peasant proprietors to emigrate for the sake of seeking a more productive soil elsewhere ?

III. Because the Ædui invited ten thousand Boii to settle in their country, does that prove that private property was unknown to them ? Not at all. The *civitas Æduorum*, which covered a considerable area and included five of our departments, might very probably have had so large an extent of public domain, or been able to find enough unoccupied land, to admit ten thousand new cultivators. Such a circumstance, following, as it does, immediately after the ravages of Ariovistus, can easily be explained, and is not the slightest evidence of communism in land.

IV. As to the custom by which a husband and wife
contributed equal shares to a common stock and
allowed the income arising from it to accumulate, I
cannot understand in what way this proves that
there was no landed property. M. de Jubainville
ingeniously explains that what was contributed
could not have consisted of land "because its
produce cannot be hoarded," and that it must have
consisted of herds of cattle, because cattle can much
more easily be set aside for a particular object. In
his long argument there is only one thing that
he overlooks, and this is that it is possible to sell the
crops and set aside the produce of the sale. Moreover,
he gives an incorrect rendering of Cæsar, VI. 19:
hujus omnis pecuniæ fructus servantur. *Pecunia,*
in legal phraseology, is used not only of money, of not
only personal property, but also of property of every
kind, including land;[1] and *fructus* does not simply mean
produce in the literal sense of the word, but revenues
of every description. Cæsar, then, is speaking of possessions of every sort, of which the income may be set
aside. These possessions may be an estate under
cultivation, or a herd of cattle, or a stock in trade, or

---

[1] Gaius iii. 124 : *Appellatione pecuniæ omnes res in lege
significantur. . . fundum vel hominem. . . . Digest,* L. 16,
222 : *pecuniæ nomine non solum numerata pecunia, sed omnes res
tam soli quam mobiles continentur.* Cf. S. Augustine, *De Discipl.
Christ.,* i.: *omnia quorum domini sumus pecunia vocantur; servus,
ager, arbor, pecus, pecunia dicitur.*

a sum of money placed out at interest (for this was not unknown to the Gauls); the income might be the produce of the sale of the crops, or the increase of the herd, or the profits of trade, or the interest on the loan. Whichever it may have been, Cæsar did not intend to imply that the Gauls were unacquainted with landed property.

I am anxious not to pass over a single argument brought forward by this learned and able writer. He observes that the names of private domains, such as we find them in the Roman and Merovingian periods, are all derived from Roman proper names. This is quite true, and I had myself made the same observation in an earlier essay; but what I had carefully abstained from saying, and what is maintained by M. de Jubainville, is that these Latin names of the Roman period prove the non-existence of domains in the Gallic period. The most they could prove is that, after the conquest, the names of domains were latinized as well as the names of individuals. Just as Gallic landowners adopted Roman names for themselves, they bestowed the same names on their estates; and consequently domains were called Pauliacus, Floriacus, Latiniacus, Avitacus, Victoriacus, etc. To conclude from this that there were no private estates before the conquest would indeed be a rash argument.

M. de Jubainville also alleges that Cæsar does not make use of the terms *villa* and *fundus* in speaking

K

of the Gauls; and he concludes from this that neither
country estates, *fundi*, nor farms, *villæ*, were to be
found in Gaul. "Before the conquest there were
neither *fundi* nor *villæ*, and the land was in common."[1]
This is another surprising statement. M. de Jubainville should not have overlooked the fact that even if
these two words do not occur in Cæsar, we find terms
which are precisely synonymous. The Romans had
more than one word to designate a country estate,
fundus, or a farm, *villa*. Instead of *fundus* they
sometimes said *ager*; and *ager* always bears this
sense in Cato, Varro, and Columella, and frequently
in Cicero and Pliny. Instead of *villa* they said
ædificium. When Varro or Columella are speaking
of the buildings standing in the midst of an estate,
they use *ædificium* as often as *villa*. Turn to the
Digest (Bk. L. Section XVI.) and compare the three
fragments 27, 60, and 211; and you will recognise
that the Romans were in the habit of calling a domain
ager and the buildings on it *ædificium*. Now Cæsar,
in speaking of the Gauls, often uses the word *agri*
and still more often *ædificia*. Here are the domains
and the *villæ* which M. de Jubainville was looking for.
These *ædificia* were farms, not huts. They contained
as a rule a somewhat numerous rural population; for
Cæsar notes in one instance as something exceptional

---

[1] *Comptes rendus de l'Académie des inscriptions*, session of
June 8, 1886, reprint, p. 6.

"that he found in the *ædificia* of the Bellovaci only a
small number of men, as almost all had set out for the
war" (viii. 7). They also included barns for the
storing of crops; for the historian mentions "that the
Tenoteri, having invaded the country of the Menapii,
supported themselves for several months on the corn
that they found in the *ædificia*" (iv. 4). The Roman
general was well aware that if he wished to find
forage for his cavalry he must look for it in those
farms, *pabulum ac ædificiis petere* (vii. 4, and viii. 10).
What Cæsar says about the *ædificium* of Ambiorix
shows that it was a large enough building to lodge a
numerous body of followers. And so the words *ager*
and *ædificium* take the place in Cæsar of the words
fundus and *villa*, and disprove the assertion that "the
Gauls had neither domains nor farms before the
conquest."

M. de Jubainville compares the whole Gallic territory with the *ager publicus* of Rome. I do not know
whether the learned medievalist has a very clear conception of what the *ager publicus* really was. The
subject is a very difficult one, and requires for its
study a good deal of time, much minute research and
great familiarity with Roman habits and customs. I
do not wish to dwell on this point; and will content
myself with saying that the *ager publicus* was not
common land, but property of the State existing side
by side with private property. To suppose that in

Gaul the State was the master of all the soil and distributed it annually amongst the citizens, is to suppose something absolutely opposed to Roman habits and to the usages of the *ager publicus.* Moreover, it is impossible to find a single line in Cæsar which authorises such a supposition.[1]

To sum up: the attempt made by this ingenious scholar to discover community in land amongst the Gauls is supported by no original authorities. When we come to verify his quotations and test his arguments, we see that not one of his quotations bears the sense he attributes to it, and that not one of his facts fits in with a theory of common ownership in land. It is wisest to keep strictly to what Cæsar tells us.

---

[1] M. de Jubainville does not translate latin texts very exactly. For example, if he sees in Cæsar that no German possesses " agri modum certum," he immediately says that " this *ager* must be the *ager publicus;* because in Rome *modus agri* was the technical expression for the *ager publicus.*" But where has he seen that? He may read in Varro, *de re rustica,* i. 14, the words *de modo agri,* which incontestably mean " concerning the extent of a private property." He will find the same expression in Varro, i. 18, where the writer says that the number of rural slaves ought to be proportionate to the extent of the domain. And again he will find the jurisconsult Paul, in the *Digest,* xviii., 1. 40, using *modum agri* for the area of an estate which an individual has just bought. To prove that *ager* by itself means *ager publicus* he cites the *lex Thoria;* without noticing that in that law the *ager publicus* is mentioned eleven times, and that *ager* does not once stand for the public land unless accompanied by *publicus* or *populi.*

Conclusion.

Are we to conclude from all that has gone before that nowhere and at no time was land held in common? By no means. To commit ourselves to so absolute a negative would be to go beyond the purpose of this work. The only conclusion to which we are brought by this prolonged examination of authorities is that community in land has not yet been historically proved. Here are scholars who have maintained that they could prove from original authorities that nations originally cultivated the soil in common; but on examining these authorities we find that they are all either incorrect, or misinterpreted, or beside the subject. M. Viollet has not brought forward a single piece of evidence which proves that the Greek cities ever practised agrarian communism. M. de Jubainville has not brought forward one which proves communism in Gaul. Maurer and Lamprecht have not produced one which shows that the mark was common land. As to the comparative method, which has been somewhat ostentatiously called into service, we are presented under its name with a strangely assorted mass of isolated facts, gathered from every quarter, and often not understood; every fact not in harmony with the theory has been left on one side. In the prosecution of what professed to be an inquiry into the domestic life of whole nations, the one thing essential has been omitted, that is, their law. In short, an imposing structure has been erected out of a series of misunderstandings. National communism has been confused with the common ownership of the family; tenure in common has been confused with ownership in common ; agrarian communism with village commons.

We do not maintain that it is inadmissible to believe in primitive communism. What we do maintain is that the attempt to base this theory on an historical foundation has been an unfortunate one; and we refuse to accept its garb of false learning.

The theory itself will always be believed in by a certain class of minds. Among the current ideas which take possession of the imaginations of men is one they have learnt from Rousseau. It is that property is contrary to nature and that communism is natural; and this idea has power even over writers who yield to it without being aware that they do so.

Minds which are under the influence of this idea will never allow that property may be a primordial fact, contemporaneous with the earliest cultivation of the soil, natural to man, produced by an instinctive recognition of his interests, and closely bound up with the primitive constitution of the family. They will always prefer to assume that there must first have been a period of communism. This will be with them an article of faith which nothing can shake ; and they will always be able to find authorities which can be made to support it. There will, however, always be a few, endowed with a keener critical and historical sense, who will continue to doubt what has yet to be proved.

However that may be, the question, in spite of so many attempts, still remains unanswered. If any one wishes to give a scientific proof of primitive communism, these are the conditions on which he may perhaps succeed:

1. He must find definite and exact authorities; which he must translate, not approximately, but with absolute correctness, according to the literal signification of the words.

2. He must abstain from adducing facts which are comparatively modern in support of an institution which he ascribes to the beginning of things, as has been done in the case of the German mark, the island of Java and the Russian *mir*.

3. He must not content himself with collecting a few isolated facts which may be exceptional; but he must study phenomena which are general, normal and far-spreading; of these he will find the evidence principally in legal records, and to a small extent in early religious customs.

4. He will be careful not to confuse agrarian communism with family ownership, which may in time become village ownership without ceasing to be a real proprietorship.

5. He will not mistake undivided tenancies on a

domain belonging to a proprietor for community in land. The fact that *villani*, who were not the owners of any land at all, often cultivated the soil in common for a lord, or annually divided it amongst themselves, has no connection with agrarian communism, and is in fact directly opposed to it.

6. He will be careful not to confuse the question by introducing village commons, unless he has first of all succeeded in proving that such commons are derived from a primitive communism. This has never yet been proved, and all that has hitherto been ascertained about commons is that they are an appendage of private property.

On these conditions alone can the work be done scientifically; short of this the only result will be a confused picture of the fancy. If any one, after taking all these precautions against gross error, discovers a body of facts and evidence in support of a theory of communism, he will have settled the question historically. Till then, do not invoke history in its favour. Present your theory as an abstract idea which may be valuable, but with which history has nothing to do. Let us not have sham learning. In saying this I have at heart the interests of historical science. There is danger lest, from love of a theory, a whole series of errors should be forcibly thrust into history. What I fear is not the theory itself; it will not affect the progress of human events; but it is the

method employed to secure its acceptance.   I distrust
this pretended application of learning, this practice of
forcing documents to say the very opposite of what
they really say, this superficial habit of talking about
all the nations of the world without having studied
a single one.   Never have "original authorities" been
so much lauded as to-day; never have they been used
with so much levity.

THE END.

SOCIAL SCIENCE SERIES.

Scarlet Cloth, each 2s. 6d.

1. **Work and Wages.** Prof. J. E. Thorold Rogers.
   " Nothing that Professor Rogers writes can fail to be of interest to thoughtful people."—*Athenæum.*

2. **Civilisation: its Cause and Cure.** Edward Carpenter.
   " No passing phase of paralism, but a permanent possession."—*Scottish Review.*

3. **Quintessence of Socialism.** Dr. Schäffle.
   " Precisely the manual needed. Brief, lucid, fair, and wise."—*British Weekly.*

4. **Darwinism and Politics.** D. G. Ritchie, M.A. (Oxon.)
   New Edition, with two additional Essays on Human Evolution.
   " One of the most suggestive books we have met with."—*Literary World.*

5. **Religion of Socialism.** E. Belfort Bax.

6. **Ethics of Socialism.** E. Belfort Bax.
   " Mr. Bax is by far the ablest of the English exponents of Socialism."—*Westminster Review.*

7. **The Drink Question.** Dr. Kate Mitchell.
   " Plenty of interesting matter for reflection."—*Graphic.*

8. **Promotion of General Happiness.** Prof. M. Macmillan.
   " A reasoned account of the most advanced and most enlightened utilitarian doctrine in a clear and readable form."—*Scotsman.*

9. **England's Ideal, &c.** Edward Carpenter.
   " The literary power is unmistakable, their freshness of style, their humour, and their enthusiasm."—*Pall Mall.*

10. **Socialism in England.** Sidney Webb, LL.B.
    " The best general view of the subject from the modern Socialist side."—*Athenæum.*

11. **Prince Bismarck and State Socialism.** W. H. Dawson.
    " A succinct well-digested review of German social and economic legislation since 1870."—*Saturday Review.*

12. **Godwin's Political Justice (On Property).**
    Edited by H. S. Salt.
    " Shows Godwin at his best; with an interesting and informing introduction."—*Glasgow Herald.*

13. **The Story of the French Revolution.** E. Belfort Bax.
    " A trustworthy outline."—*Scotsman.*

14. **The Co-Operative Commonwealth.** Laurence Gronlund.
    " An independent exposition of the Socialism of the Marx School."—*Contemporary Review.*

15. **Essays and Addresses.** Bernard Bosanquet, M.A. (Oxon.)
    " Ought to be in the hands of every student of the Nineteenth Century spirit."—*Echo.*
    " No one can complain of not being able to understand what Mr. Bosanquet means."—*Pall Mall Gazette.*
    [turn ov]

SOCIAL SCIENCE SERIES—*Continued.*

16. **Charity Organisation.**
C. S. LOCH, Secretary to Charity Organisation Society.
" A perfect little manual."—*Athenæum.*
" Deserves a wide circulation."—*Scotsman.*

17. **Thoreau's Anti-Slavery and Reform Papers.**
Edited by H. S. SALT.
" An interesting collection of essays."—*Literary World.*

18. **Self-Help a Hundred Years Ago.** G J. HOLYOAKE.
" Will be studied with much benefit by all who are interested in the amelioration of the condition of the poor."—*Morning Post.*

19. **The New York State Reformatory at Elmira.**
ALEXANDER WINTER ; with Preface by HAVELOCK ELLIS.
" A valuable contribution to the literature of penology."—*Black and White.*

20. **Common-sense about Women.** T. W. HIGGINSON.
" An admirable collection of papers, advocating in the most liberal spirit the emancipation of women."—*Woman's Herald.*

21. **The Unearned Increment.** W. H. DAWSON.
" A concise but comprehensive volume."—*Echo.*

22. **Our Destiny.** LAURENCE GRONLUND.
" A very vigorous little book, dealing with the influence of socialism on morals and religion."—*Daily Chronicle.*

23. **The Working-Class Movement in America.**
Dr. EDWARD and E. MARX AVELING.
" Will give a good idea of the condition of the working classes in America, and of the various organizations which they have formed."—*Scots Leader.*

24. **Luxury.** EMILE DE LAVELEYE.
" An eloquent plea on moral and economical grounds for simplicity of life."
—*Academy.*

25. **The Land and the Labourers.** Rev. C. W. STUBBS, M.A.
" This admirable book should be circulated in every village in the country. '
—*Manchester Guardian.*

26. **The Evolution of Property.** PAUL LAFARGUE.
" Will prove interesting and profitable to all students of economic history."
—*Scotsman.*

27. **Crime and its Causes.** W. DOUGLAS MORRISON.
" Can hardly fail to suggest to all readers several new and pregnant reflections on the subject."—*Anti-Jacobin.*

28. **Principles of State Interference.**
D. G. RITCHIE, M.A. (Oxon.)
" An interesting contribution to the controversy on the functions of the State."—*Glasgow Herald.*

29. **German Socialism and F. Lassalle.** W. H. DAWSON.
" As a biographical history of German socialistic movements during this century, it may be accepted as complete."—*British Weekly.*

30. **The Purse and the Conscience.** H. M. THOMPSON, B.A.
" Shows common sense and fairness in his arguments."—*Scotsman.*

[OVER

OTHER VOLUMES IN PREPARATION.

Origin of Property in Land. Fustel de Coulanges. Edited, with an Introductory Chapter on the English Manor, by Prof. J. W. Ashley, M.A.

The Co-Operative Movement.   Beatrice Potter.

The English Republic.
W. J. Linton. Edited by Kineton Parker.

Modern Humanists.   J. M. Robertson.

Neighbourhood Guilds.   Dr. Stanton Coit.

The Impossibility of Social Democracy.   Dr. Schaffle.

Collectivism and Socialism.
A. Nacquet. Edited by W. Heaford.

The Labour Problem.   Lange. Edited by Rev. J. Carter.

Progress and Prospects of Political Economy.
Prof. J. K. Ingram.

The London Programme.   Sidney Webb.

The Destitute Alien in England.   Arnold White and others.

The Revolutionary Spirit.
M. Rocquain. Edited by J. D. Hunting.

Outlooks from a New Standpoint.   E. Belfort Bax.

University Extension.   M. E. Sadler.

Criminal Anthropology.
M. C. Lombroso. Edited by R. F. Crawford.

Co-Operative Societies.
Prof. Pizzamiglio. Edited by F. J. Snell.

Communism and Anarchism.   R. W. Burnie.

Malthus' Essay on Population.   Abridged by A. K. Donald.

The Student's Marx: an Introduction to his "Capital."

— — — —   —

SWAN SONNENSCHEIN & CO., LONDON.

POLITICAL BOOKLETS.

A Short History of Parliament. By B. C. Skottowe, M A. Second Edition. Crown 8vo, cloth, 2s 6d.

Mr. Chamberlain writes :—" Some account, in a popular form, of the working of our greatest representative institution has been much wanted, and you seem to me to have fulfilled your task with skill and success. I hope that you may be rewarded by a large circulation."

" Presents a great amount of valuable information in a lucid fashion and in a very small compass."—*Scotsman.*

" It deals very carefully and completely with this side of Constitutional History."—*Spectator.*

" This historical survey of 336 pages covers an immense space of ground, beginning with the Witan and ending with Mr. Biggar."—*Pall Mall Gazette.*

" Clear, lively, and anecdotic."—*St. James's Gazette.*

The Rules, Customs, and Procedure of the House of Commons. By Charles Bradlaugh, M.P. Fcap. 8vo, half-bound in paper boards, 2s 6d.

" A good book, and admirably brief."—*Spectator.*

" It is a useful and serviceable little book."—*Athenæum.*

" A most excellent little handbook to Parliamentary practice."—*Academy.*

Lord Randolph Churchill. A Study of English Democracy. By Dr. J. B. Crozier, author of "Civilization and Progress," etc. Crown 8vo, cloth, 2s.

' The writer makes out his case that a more dangerous demagogue than Lord Randolph, one more guiltless of true statesmanship, indeed more indifferent to anything but the applause of the masses, does not exist. . . . It is in relation to the philosophy of democracy that we think the volume so useful and so worthy of attention. . . . Dr. Crozier's study of the general ways and tricks of demagogues is extremely good."—*Spectator.*

" The most severe and pitiless vivisection of a public man which we remember ever to have seen."—*Scotsman.*

Home Rule and the Irish Question. By the Right Hon. Joseph Chamberlain, M.P. An authorized edition of Mr. Chamberlain's Irish speeches. Issued under the auspices of the National Radical Union. With a new Portrait of Mr. Chamberlain. Crown 8vo, cloth neat, 2s ; or paper wrappers, 1s.

Speeches on the Irish Question. By the Right Hon. Joseph Chamberlain, M.P. Issued under the auspices of the National Liberal Union, Birmingham. With a new Portrait of Mr. Chamberlain. Crown 8vo, cloth neat, 2s ; or paper wrappers, 1s.

A Unionist Policy for Ireland. Being a series of articles originally contributed to the *Birmingham Daily Post.* With a Preface by the Right Hon. Joseph Chamberlain, M.P. Issued under the auspices of the National Radical Union. In paper wrapper, Crown 8vo, 1s.

" A solid contribution to the discussion of that problem which is still agitating the politics of Great Britain."—*Evening Post.*

SWAN SONNENSCHEIN & CO., LONDON.

www.ingramcontent.com/pod-product-compliance
Lightning Source LLC
Chambersburg PA
CBHW030827270326
41928CB00007B/936